The Dream of
Christian Socialism
An Essay on Its European Origins

Bernard Murchland

The Dream of Christian Socialism
An Essay on Its European Origins

Bernard Murchland

American Enterprise Institute for Public Policy Research
Washington and London

Bernard Murchland, professor of philosophy at Ohio Wesleyan University, has written many books and articles on religious and existential thought. He is the editor of *Antaeus,* a newsletter for the humanities.

Library of Congress Cataloging in Publication Data

Murchland, Bernard.
   The dream of Christian socialism.

   (AEI studies ; 343)
   Bibliography: p. 73
   1. Socialism—Europe—History.   2. Socialism.
3. Democracy.   I. Title.   II. Series.
HX237.M86   335'.7'094   81–14919
ISBN 0–8447–3470–5   AACR2

AEI Studies 343

Printed in the United States of America

Contents

In our present state a division of possessions is necessary since community of possessions is a source of strife. In the state of innocence, however, without any danger of strife they would have used in common, according to each one's need, those things of which they were the masters.

— THOMAS AQUINAS

Every time one expects to encounter brotherhood one bumps into terror.

— JEAN-PAUL SARTRE

Christian socialism is but the holy water with which the priest consecrates the heart-burnings of the aristocrat.

— KARL MARX

Preface

My aim in this study has been twofold. I first attempt to synthesize the vast materials on the origins of Christian socialism in Europe. Second, I offer a critical perspective on its development. I relate Christian socialism incidentally to the larger history of social reform. My treatment is far from exhaustive, but it attempts to deal with the major figures and themes. The roots of Christian socialism go far back into history. I have begun my analysis with the nineteenth century because that is when the term "socialism" emerges as a distinct concept.

Socialism remains a major option for twentieth-century nations and continues to generate much of our political dialogue. It may be, as some claim, that capitalism is exhausted, but that is far from clear. And, even if capitalism has had its day, it is by no means certain that socialism is its natural heir. Although capitalism has not, to be sure, solved all our problems, it does not follow that socialism can. The socialist Michael Harrington is fond of saying that socialism has never been given a chance in America. He may be right. But socialism has been tried over and over again in Europe, with dubious results. In most cases it has not succeeded very well, and where it has succeeded it is unpalatable to those with democratic instincts. Thus there is a constant note of expectation in the writings of socialists themselves. They await a day of fuller realization, a kind of secular Parousia in which things now dimly perceived will be revealed in great glory by the dialectic of history.

So socialism is more an ideal than a reality, as it always has been. I confess that it is an attractive one. I have always been sympathetic to most of the ends socialists seek but have become increasingly critical of the means they propose. I too believe in a fuller humanity—more equality, more freedom, more justice—but I reject statism as a means of obtaining it. I also have questions about some socialistic premises, as will become evident in the text. Daniel Bell has described himself as a socialist in economics, a liberal in politics, and a conservative in culture. I see myself rather as a liberal (or perhaps a neoliberal) in economics, more a conservative than not in politics, and a socialist in culture. It seems to me the socialist ideals of community and equality can be more readily achieved in the sphere of culture than anywhere else. I at any rate find more fellowship in theater rehearsals or at sporting events than in economic and political transactions.

I hope this little opus will be accepted as a contribution to the ongoing dialogue.

Introduction: A Short History of Christian Socialism

In 1848 the flames of revolution threatened to consume the entire continent of Europe. Old regimes were tumbling; powerful new forces were struggling onto the stage of history. The cry everywhere was for social transformation—at any cost, by any means—and the price of progress was most often paid in blood. Karl Marx, whose *Communist Manifesto* appeared in that year, issued the battle call by urging support "for every revolutionary movement against the existing social and political order of things."[1]

France, as had become her custom, was the center of the revolutionary spirit. On February 24, 1848, Parisians took to the barricades once more. The clever but fumbling Louis Philippe was forced to abdicate. A new republic was proclaimed that was more sympathetic to democratic demands. The socialist Louis Blanc was given a cabinet position in the new government and on his initiative national workshops (*associations ouvrières*) were instituted to create more jobs for the working classes. Idealism was again let loose in the land, emotions glowed, and trees of liberty were planted in the parks. Fittingly, the poet Lamartine headed the Second Republic—the Lamartine who had written *La Chute d'un ange* [the fall of an angel]. But on June 23 the people staged yet another insurrection, and Lamartine was out of office. In those unsettled times, angels fell rapidly.

One of the keenest observers in the streets of Paris during the February Revolution was a young Englishman named John Malcolm Ludlow. He had been born in India and had spent his youth in France before returning to England in 1838. He was nine when the Revolution of 1830 overthrew the last of the Bourbons. Early in life Ludlow developed strong religious convictions, which he combined

[1] Karl Marx and Frederick Engels *The Communist Manifesto* (New York: International Publishers, 1948), p. 44.

with a keen interest in social problems. These interests from the beginning were radically democratic. Ludlow regarded himself as "a man of the people" and opposed the inequality of any form of society that favored hierarchy and privilege. His radicalism derived in part from his liberal Protestant upbringing and in part from the romantic literature of the day, in which he was well versed. Victor Hugo was one of his favorite authors. In addition, Ludlow was familiar with the ideas of Robert Owen, the duc de Saint-Simon, and François Fourier, as well as those of Joseph Buchez and Robert Lamennais—ideas that were very much in the air while he was a student in Paris. Their conception of equality and cooperation, he wrote in his diary, "was one of the great discoveries of the century."[2]

[2] John Malcolm Ludlow, quoted in Torben Christensen, *Origin and History of Christian Socialism 1848–54* (Copenhagen: Universitetsforlaget I Aarhus, 1962), p. 40. This well-researched book was my principal source of information about the early Christian socialist movement in England. I also acknowledge a debt to Charles E. Raven, *Christian Socialism 1848–1854* (New York: Augustus M. Kelley, Publishers, 1968).

1

England

The England to which the young Ludlow returned was scarcely a seedbed of revolution, but neither was it immune from the currents of unrest sweeping over the rest of Europe. In fact, as Max Beer has pointed out in his noted study, the British were since the thirteenth century major contributors to the current of socialist thought and reform.[1] By 1838 Robert Owen's ideas had worked their way into the thinking of labor reformers. Among other signs of the times could be counted the numerous dissenting religious groups, especially the Quakers and Methodists, who were lending their support to reform movements. The nonconformist sects provided most of the leaders for the trade union movement from about 1815 onward, and the Wesleyan revival was a major influence on eighteenth-century social reform in England. It has been claimed that the founders of Methodism were the spiritual ancestors of the labor leaders.[2] A renewal of theology had also been launched by the Tractarians, stressing the incarnational and sacramental aspects of Christianity, although the Tractarians were only indirectly social reformers.

The "romantic protest" was also at full sail during this time. Samuel Taylor Coleridge (who has been called "the first voice of Christian socialism"), Robert Southey, Thomas Carlyle, and others were lamenting the spiritual poverty of the new industrial order. The romantics were also an important conduit for German idealism. Perhaps the most significant reform effort of the period was to be found in the Chartist movement which had begun in 1836 as an agency for improving the lot of the working class. In 1838 the People's Charter, comprising six points (including universal manhood suf-

[1] Max Beer, *A History of British Socialism*, vol. I (London: G. Bell & Sons, 1919), p. v.
[2] Gilbert C. Binyon, *The Christian Socialist Movement in England* (New York: The Macmillan Company, 1931), p. 24.

1

frage), was drawn up. Ludlow himself could not at this time be described as a social activist, though he did play a minor role in the British India Society and the Anti–Corn Law League. After his return to England he had taken up the study of law but was not yet sure what direction his life might take.

A turning point came in 1844 when A. P. Stanley's *Life and Correspondence of Thomas Arnold* appeared. Ludlow read it in thrall, finding in Arnold just the right blend of religious conviction and social radicalism. Stanley's *Life*, according to Torben Christensen,

> became the starting point for his subsequent idea of Christian Socialism and its tasks. . . . Ludlow realized that social issues were of the utmost importance and that all efforts ought to be directed to the extirpation of the evils of society. This meant, above all, releasing the working classes from all social and economic bondage, with its ensuing moral and intellectual degradation, and elevating them to the state of free, responsible citizens.[3]

Arnold's decisive influence was reinforced in the summer of 1846 when, on a visit to Paris, Ludlow met the Lutheran pastor Louis Meyer. He was impressed with Meyer's evangelical spirit and even more with his efforts on behalf of the poor. Meyer had founded an organization called La Société des Amis des Pauvres, which gave Ludlow the first clue to his own vocation in life. He returned to London resolved to work with the poor. His first thought was to enlist some of his colleagues at Lincoln's Inn where he had studied law. In the course of carrying out this plan he was advised to seek the help of the chaplain at Lincoln's Inn. Thus, Ludlow came to meet Frederick Denison Maurice, whom he later described as one of the three greatest influences on his life. Arnold and Meyer were the other two. To these men, he wrote in his autobiography, "I owe under God my better self."[4]

As it happened this first encounter between Maurice and Ludlow was rather unpromising. Maurice was polite but reserved and unencouraging. A number of reasons have been given for Maurice's lack of interest. He was, for one thing, in mourning for his recently deceased wife. For another, he was much occupied with his duties as chaplain and newly appointed professor of divinity at King's College. But the real reason would appear to be a failure of sympathy with Ludlow's ideas, stemming from an inability to grasp them intellectually. Maurice's social thinking was far in arrears of Ludlow's.

---

[3] Torben Christensen, *Origin and History of Christian Socialism 1848–54* (Copenhagen: Universitetsforlaget I Aarhus, 1962), p. 53.

[4] Quoted in ibid., p. 52.

He was, after all, a theologian, and one well known, who did not believe that social work of the kind Ludlow proposed was compatible with his calling.

Maurice's primary concern when he met Ludlow was, and would ever remain, religion. He was born a Unitarian; he converted to the Church of England in 1831; and he was ordained three years later. While a student at Cambridge, he was a member of the Apostle's Club and early formed an idealistic conception of human nature, principally under the influence of Plato and Coleridge. The leading themes of his theology—divine order, fellowship, the law of love, and so forth—were not, to be sure, without political consequences. Maurice always opposed an atomistic view of society and held advanced views on equality. In March 1840, he wrote an article on Chartism and acknowledged that there was a serious problem with the working class. But, typically, he saw it as a religious rather than a social problem. What the workers needed, he argued, was education in the basic tenets of catechism. The church, in other words, held the answer to the questions raised by Chartism. Maurice was always willing to support educational efforts for the poor. But he stopped short of taking more concrete action—of dirtying his hands, to use a latter-day expression.

This, then, was the Maurice that Ludlow had met in the summer of 1846. When they met again in April 1848, circumstances had altered Maurice's outlook. Ludlow had returned from the February Revolution in Paris overcome with a sense of the enormity of the social crisis and fired with resolve to Christianize the socialist movement. He recorded these words in his autobiography:

> For myself, the sight of all I saw around me in France impressed on me the conviction, on the one hand that this was an essentially socialistic revolution, the principles of which would spread from France throughout the world, and on the other hand that socialism must be made Christian to be a blessing for France and for the world.[5]

It may be true that the English on the whole did not fear the spread of the revolution to their own shores. Still, they had much to be concerned about. The Paris outbreak had given renewed life to the Chartist cause. A series of crop failures and economic crises during "the hungry forties" had worsened the plight of English workers. They wondered why they too could not have instant redress as their French brethren did. The Chartists organized to march on Parliament on April 10, 1848, with a petition of demands. No one

[5] Ibid., p. 61.

could deny that things might get out of hand. Troops were called in, and a large force of constables was deputized. As it turned out, the demonstration fizzled out, and the public peace was not disturbed. But by their action the Chartists had incurred the wrath of a large public and were not thereafter a politically effective body.

The Chartist uprising convinced Maurice that some action must be taken. That same evening he met with Ludlow and Charles Kingsley to discuss what might be done. They issued a proclamation expressing solidarity with the workers and agreed to publish a newspaper, which appeared on May 6 as *Politics for the People*. Maurice and Ludlow were coeditors. In the first issue Maurice pledged to discuss the issues of the day "from a Christian point of view" and acknowledged that liberty, fraternity, and equality are intended for all. Maurice had come a long way from his previous position. But he was far from a firebrand. He interpreted the revolutionary slogan in a conservative, essentially theological manner. The virtues of liberty, equality, and fraternity were not to be had by overthrowing the existing order, but by recognizing that they are already available in Christian teaching. Maurice still read the situation through religious lenses.

Kingsley's role in the Christian socialist movement is more difficult to assess, but it was an important one. Charles E. Raven writes that "he was for a long time its chief spokesman, and in addition supplied the motive power for its first enterprise. If Maurice was the man of vision, the Moses of Christian Socialism, Kingsley with his power of tongue and pen can claim to be its Aaron."[6] Although Kingsley had neither the erudition of Maurice nor the organizational skills of Ludlow, he was certainly an enthusiastic and sympathetic colleague and was particularly valuable to the cause as a propagandist.

Ludlow, however, was the principal contributor to the paper. It was he who pressed the issue of socialism. He had a greater empirical sense than Maurice, was more in sympathy with the democratic spirit, and was besides much more conversant with socialist writings. Maurice had very little stomach for socialism or any form of democracy. As late as 1866, one year before the New Reform Bill was passed, Maurice expressed his distaste for "the will of the majority." This was an early cause of a rift between him and Ludlow. The latter wanted Maurice to take more initiative in publishing articles on socialism. Maurice, however, preferred to discuss education.

Politics for the People folded after a few weeks, without seeming

<hr>

[6] Charles E. Raven, *Christian Socialism 1848–1854* (New York: Augustus M. Kelley, Publishers, 1968), pp. 93–94.

4

to have had much effect. But it signaled a change in the religious consciousness of the time and brought together three remarkable men, bound by bonds of uncommon religious fervor and a desire for social improvement. These three formed the energetic nucleus of the Christian socialist movement. The record of their achievements was considerable and was to have a lasting influence on English society. They formed study clubs, recruited new colleagues, conducted classes in the London slums, crusaded for sanitary reform, published at great length, formed a Society for Promoting Working Men's Associations (which led to the founding of dozens of producers' cooperatives), and eventually established a working men's college—all in the short space of seven years! In the course of these activities they clarified their thinking and honed their organizational techniques. Socialism was for them first and foremost a religious movement; their aim was to win the working classes for Christianity. Their signal contribution was to emphasize certain neglected aspects of the social teachings of the church. In this they were greatly indebted to Ludlow's familiarity with socialist thought and Maurice's theology. Socialism as they understood it did not mean the reform of society on socialistic principles so much as the realignment of socialism to conform with Christian principles. As Maurice was fond of saying, the aim of the movement was to Christianize the unchristian socialists and socialize the unsocial Christians.

A fairly clear sense of how the Christian socialists were thinking can be gathered from this declaration that accompanied the formation of the Society for Promoting Working Men's Associations:

> It is now our business to show by what machinery the objects of Christian socialism can, as we believe, be compassed; how working men can release themselves, and can be helped by others to release themselves, from the thraldom of individual labour under the competitive system; or at least how far they can, at present, by honest fellowship, mitigate its evils. In offering this machinery to others, we are bound to protest against that idolatry of social mechanism, which imagines society as a mere assemblage of wheels and springs, and not as a partnership of living men, which takes account of the form alone, and not of the spirit which animates it; but we have also to protest with scarcely less of earnestness against that idolatry of individual will, which scorns all regular means of action—looks for all social improvements to the mere genius of some mighty leader in whose way it would almost place obstacles, like hurdles, for him to leap over, rather than smooth the way for the feebler crowd; or against that faith which sees God only in

the works of nature, and not in the works of men; which may delight in tracing the harmonies of the solar system, yet sees nothing but human devices and intellectual snares in the harmonies of social organization; which acknowledges as divine the instinctive laws of a community of bees or of emmets, but turns away from the laws of a fellowship of men as if they had nothing to do with the will, with the wisdom, with the love, of the Great Law-giver.[7]

In the first tract on Christian socialism (February 1850), Maurice declared: "I seriously believe that Christianity is the only foundation of Socialism, and that a true Socialism is the necessary result of a sound Christianity." Fellowship and cooperation were the precepts of the new movement, against the competitive spirit of capitalism. Maurice argued that if God's order was one body having many members, and if fellowship and cooperation are the ground of the divine order, then socialism is the foundation of society. Still, it was a pious and rather abstract socialism that did not imply any basic changes in the economic order. It did not imply revolution, the abolition of private property, collectivism, equal incomes, joint ownership, or the supremacy of the working class, and certainly not materialism or atheism. As Christensen puts it, socialism meant for Maurice "demonstrating that the ideas of brotherhood, fellowship, and fellow-work as the essence of socialism, expressed the laws of God's universe."[8]

Maurice was as much troubled by the delinquency of the church as by the plight of the workers. The church, he felt, had lost the true sense of being the body of Christ; it conceded too much to the individualism rampant in society and identified too exclusively with the privileged classes. But Maurice's logic was an accommodating one: it postulated the existing monarchy as the foundation of socialism. Maurice appealed to the principle of subordination in the Trinity: he reasoned that the conflict between master and slave could never be abolished but only set in right order by the principles of socialism. In the deep theological waters Maurice was wont to ply, true humanity lay beneath all isms and social arrangements. Ludlow always agreed with Maurice that Christianity was the spiritual ground of socialism. They shared, too, a common missionary goal of conquering the working masses for Christ. But Maurice's uncompromising theological posture was from the beginning an important difference between them.

[7] Binyon, *Christian Socialist Movement*, p. 228.
[8] Christensen, *Origin and History of Christian Socialism*, p. 137.

On November 2, 1850, Ludlow became editor of a new periodical, *The Christian Socialist*, which furnished him a forum for expounding his own views more freely. In the first issue he proclaimed that Christian socialism was meant "to vindicate for Christianity its true authority over the realms of industry and trade, for Socialism its true character as the great Christian revolution of the nineteenth century." Maurice could agree with this statement so long as it did not stray from a strict theological interpretation. But for Ludlow it pointed in directions Maurice could not follow; it connoted changes in the social order that were abhorrent to him. Ludlow continued to be influenced by French doctrines of association. He meant by socialism a planned economy, the abolition of the distinction between capitalists and workers, self-government, an end to class distinction and privilege, and, indeed, the abolition of private property. As he confessed in the same issue of *The Christian Socialist:* "So long as each labors for all as all labor for him, and endeavors always to do his best, because he knows that he will receive the best that can be given him, Communism, pure Communism, will I feel sure, exhibit the very type of a flourishing society."

A showdown between Maurice and Ludlow was inevitable. There were a number of clashes before the final split in 1855, when the Society for Promoting Working Men's Associations was dissolved. They disagreed, for example, whether or not unbelievers could work in the Christian socialist movement. As a result of this dispute Ludlow resigned his editorship of *The Christian Socialist* and Maurice moved immediately to change the name of the paper. There were other confrontations as well. Maurice had always been edgy about Ludlow's radicalism and used his considerable skills as an infighter to cast the movement in a more moderate light. Ludlow, for his part, accused Maurice of a concerted effort to betray the principles of Christian socialism. Issues became partisan; sides formed; tension and strife wracked the small group. To add to all of these difficulties Maurice fell under censure for his theological views and was dismissed from King's College in October 1853 (though later, in 1864, he would be given a chair of Moral Philosophy at Cambridge). Maurice thereupon threw himself into a project to create a workingmen's college. He had all along held dearly to the notion of a divine order underlying all forms of social organization. The college was to be the instrument of this belief. Curiously, it was also to spell the end of Christian socialism as a movement.

Maurice's interest in the cooperatives, never very great, was now completely eclipsed by his enthusiasm for the new college. As Peter Jones notes in his fine study:

He was in constant fear that the cooperative associations were absorbing too much time and energy and diverting his little band away from what he thought to be its main work—the proclamation of the already existing Divine order. Maurice's theology was thus never fully consonant with the associationist-socialist work of Christian socialism, and he began to focus efforts on adult education instead.[9]

The misunderstanding between Maurice and Ludlow was now complete. Ludlow records these bittersweet lines in his autobiography: "I had willfully blinded myself. . . . The Maurice I had devoted myself to was a Maurice of my own imagination, not the real Maurice. He was not to blame, I was. . . . So Mr. Maurice had his way, and the comparatively broad stream of Christian socialism was turned into the narrow channel of a Working Men's College."[10] Yet Ludlow, who seems always to have been virtually mesmerized by Maurice's personality, collaborated faithfully in the new project.

Maurice died in 1872. Ludlow died in 1911 at the age of ninety-one, somewhat eclipsed, but never a broken man. He remained active in the socialist cause, particularly trade unionism, published articles and books, agitated on behalf of the North during the American Civil War, and became an influential bureaucrat in 1870 when he was appointed chief registrar of Friendly Societies. In the 1880s and 1890s when Christian socialism was revived, Ludlow participated. He served, for example, on the executive committee of the Church Socialist Union from 1891 to 1903. In 1908 he addressed the Pan-Anglican Conference, recalling for his audience Maurice's deep faith, which had animated Christian socialists over a half century ago.

Scott Holland draws this portrait of Ludlow in a fond memoir:

At the monthly meetings you would often see there a bent figure sitting with the face of one who had come out of other more heroic days. There was a nobility in the prophetic head which made the rest of us look very cheap. And now and again when some pink, youthful, cheerful pessimist . . . had plunged us all into the abyss of despair, the old man would rise and shake with the passion of old days that forever haunted him with their wickedness and woe, and bid us cheer up. . . . The fire still gleamed in his eyes so that they shone with the passionate light which is only to be seen in men who have known Maurice. He quivered with an underground, volcanic vehemence which no years

---

[9] Peter d'A. Jones, *The Christian Socialist Revival 1877–1914* (Princeton: Princeton University Press, 1968), p. 27. This is the best treatment of Christian socialism in the late nineteenth century and contains an excellent bibliography.

[10] Quoted in Christensen, *Origin and History of Christian Socialism*, p. 364.

8

or grey hairs could tame; he was devoured by a great zeal for justice. We felt we were listening to the man Maurice found so hard to hold. . . . A deep, strong, noble soul, he retained to the last his democratic faith in the people, his passionate pity for the poor and downtrodden, his fiery cry for righteousness.[11]

Ludlow's self-evaluation of his career is considerably more subdued. He had never regarded himself as first rate in anything he did. He thought of himself rather as "God's handyman, pushing a bit here and pulling there."[12] It is tempting to wonder how the course of Christian socialism might have gone had Ludlow been able to combine his brilliant intellectual gifts with Maurice's charisma and qualities of leadership! As it was, his impact was a major one. Gilbert Binyon pays him this compliment: "It is to be noted that . . . largely through Ludlow's influence, there has been in England a comparative absence of that complete alienation between organized Religion and the Socialist Movement which is all too common in the rest of the world."[13]

Against the Industrial System

There was not to be another organized Christian socialist body until 1877 when Stewart Duckworth Headlam founded the Guild of Saint Matthew. Since Headlam had been a student of Maurice's at Cambridge the guild may be regarded as a direct descendant of the earlier group of Christian socialists. Thus it is not surprising that the guild was founded for the purpose of combating atheism and revivifying the spirit of religion both in the church and among the people. One of its members, Dean (later Bishop) Charles Stubbs, said in an unmistakable Maurician voice that a better order of society was evolving according to a divine plan. Another, Thomas Hancock, preached a widely hailed sermon entitled "The Banner of Christ is in the Hands of the Socialists."

The immediate cause of the rebirth of Christian socialism was a recurrence of social crisis. From about 1870 onward England was shaken by a series of strikes, economic depressions, and general social unrest. The 1880s was a particularly stormy decade when passions boiled and tempers flared in countless demonstrations, capped

---

[11] Scott Holland, *A Bundle of Memories*, quoted in Neville C. Masterman, *John Malcolm Ludlow: The Builder of Christian Socialism* (Cambridge: The University Press, 1963), p. 250.

[12] Quoted in ibid., p. 254.

[13] Binyon, *Christian Socialist Movement*, p. 84.

9

in 1889 by a six-week dock strike. Many socialists groups were organized during this period. In 1883 the Land Reform Union came into existence, and in 1884 such important groups as the Fabians, the Social Democratic Federation, and the Socialist League were formed. Thus Headlam's initiative in founding the Guild of St. Matthew was not merely a response to the social crisis; it was as well an initiation of similar efforts all over England.

Headlam inherited from Maurice a theology that was strongly reformist and sacramental in character. The eucharist, he believed, was the sacrament of unity, and baptism the sacrament of brotherhood and equality. With Maurice, he held that Christianity not only implied socialism but was its very foundation. For Headlam, Christianity was a thoroughly democratic religion. He said in one of his sermons,

> I would ask you to bear in mind that the character of this Society, the Christian Church, is distinctly and essentially democratic; its founder, Jesus Christ, was, at any rate, a Carpenter, who became a radical reformer both in social and religious matters—we, members of the Society believe, as we think on good grounds, that so, radical reform received not only human but divine sanction.[14]

And in his address to the annual meeting of the guild in 1883 he postulated a direct connection between faith and political activism:

> In the worship of Jesus really present in the Sacrament of the Altar before you, all human hearts can join, and especially secularists, for when you worship Him you are worshipping the Savior, the social and political Emancipator, the greatest of all secular workers, the founder of the great Socialistic society for the promotion of righteousness, the preacher of a revolution, the denouncer of kings, the gentle, tender sympathizer with the rough and the outcast, who could utter scathing, burning words against the rich, the respectable, the religious.[15]

Thus the dynamic of the guild was centrifugal, wafting outward to society from a strong sacramental core. The intended outcome was a better distribution of wealth and a greater measure of self-government. Binyon offers this helpful summary:

> It may be well here to add a word or two in further explanation of what the Maurice-Headlam school taught (and teaches). It is indebted, not only to Maurice and Headlam, but also to men like Farquhar and Pulsford. It interprets

[14] Ibid., p. 120.
[15] Ibid., p. 122.

10

Catholicism in the light of what may be called a divine-humanist, spiritual-materialist, social-democratic philosophy of life generally. Thus, for example, the essential truth about mankind is that it is the family and mystical Body of God. The Church is the Sacrament of that universal and essential fact—its outward sign and witness, and the means of helping men to effectualise it. So, again, all men are God's priests. That universal and essential fact is manifested and specially focused in that priestly democracy, the Church, and in its official priesthood—which for the sake of "holy order" is, for certain functions, the Church's mouthpiece. Similarly, the declared Real Presence of the Eternal Christ beneath the bread and wine of the Mass is the focused manifestation of the essential fact that "in Him all things consist," and that as those representative products of God's earth, bread and wine, consecrated by mankind's representative, the Church, to be shared in holy Communion, manifests the Christ, so will the whole world and its products manifest Him in whom they consist when they are used and shared by all mankind in the holy Communism for which the race is created. And because that Communism will be a life of which beauty will be an essential ingredient, therefore the symbol and foretaste of that life, the Mass, should be celebrated with the utmost possible beauty of colour and sound and scent and movement. This interpretation of the Mass reveals how inseparable, from this point of view, religion and politics must always be. Belief in Communism (in the essential meaning of that word)—that is, a world-order in which no owning and exploiting class stands between the people and their access to "the means of production, distribution, and exchange," and in which those things are used by all as free men, free groups, and free nations, in some form of co-operation for the common good—this belief is no mere "extra" or permissible "pious opinion," *but is of the very essence of the Catholic Faith.*[16]

Although Headlam shared much of Maurice's theology, he was a very different personality. Maurice was puritanical and private; Headlam was colorful and irrepressibly gregarious, indeed bohemian. His lighthearted ways kept him in hot water with church authorities most of the time. Headlam served with George Bernard Shaw on the executive committee of the Fabian Society (and became one of the models for Morell in Shaw's play *Candida*). He was a frequenter of pubs and a master heckler at meetings, and he em-

---

[16] Ibid., pp. 202–3. My emphasis. Note the easy transition from Communion to Communism. It should be pointed out that this theology is more Headlam than Maurice.

braced with total passion such causes as the single tax (he was a close friend of Henry George, the American promoter of this plan), secular education, and church reform. One of his favorite causes was the defense of the rights of chorus girls. In a sermon he advised parents to send their dull children to the theater, where they could be inspired by the dancers. There is a marvelous story about Headlam arguing with the bishop about the proper color of a ballerina's thighs. Headlam regarded the dance, and the theatrical profession in general, as a quasi-sacramental sign of inward grace. He founded a church-and-stage guild and later the Shakespeare League for Children. The Guild of St. George attracted substantial support from London performers and noted authors, such as Shaw and Oscar Wilde.

Despite his idiosyncracies, which drew such embarrassing epithets as "the dancing parson" and "the Pied Piper of Bethnal Green," Headlam retained a remarkable singleness of purpose and a resolutely theological outlook. His fundamental beliefs are conveniently summed up in one of the Fabian tracts he wrote—No. 42, "Christian Socialism," published in 1892—and later elaborated in his book *The Socialist's Church*. His religious and social concerns met in the great themes of Christ's humanity, the this-worldliness of the kingdom of heaven, brotherhood and equality, and the primacy of personhood. Most people differed with Headlam, but few could deny his integrity or his deep commitment. After Headlam's death the Archbishop of Canterbury wrote that he had always marched bravely in obedience to his conscience.

Headlam, of course, made many mistakes. Two of them seriously limited the effectiveness of the guild and hastened its demise. A tactical error was his opposition to the Independent Labor Party. There are shades here of the Maurice who hated systems of all kinds and who protested the Reform Act of 1867. In November 1893, Headlam wrote in *The Church Reformer*, the official organ of the guild (which Shaw called one of the best socialist journals of the day), to express strong opposition to admitting working men into Parliament, as the Fabians advocated. Two years later he was still on the attack. It was a fatal mistake because not only did it cost him many important friends, among the Fabians and elsewhere, but also it was evidence that he misread one of the important signs of the times. He failed to estimate the grassroots strength of the labor movement, especially in the provinces. Shortly afterward *The Church Reformer* ceased publication. There is an ironic parallel here with its distant predecessor, *Politics for the People*. Both failed to reach their intended working-class audience.

12

Headlam's second mistake was to stand bail for Oscar Wilde in 1895. He did so out of generous motives, but it was a costly act. "I was surety," Headlam later explained, "not for his character but for his appearance in court to stand trial. I had very little personal knowledge of him at the time; I think I had only met him twice."[17] Oddly enough, Headlam was right about Wilde whereas he had been wrong about the ILP. Wilde was savaged by both the public and the courts, and Headlam's gesture was by any measure one of great courage. He was on hand to meet Wilde when he was released from jail two years later and wrote touchingly of that occasion: "I like to think of him as I knew him for those six hours on that spring morning and to hope that somewhere and somehow the beauty of his character may be garnered and the follies and weaknesses burnt up."[18]

The Philosophy of Freedom

In the judgment of Peter Jones, "Stewart Headlam and his disciples were the shock troops of sacramental socialism. The Christian Social Union was the army of occupation."[19] The union was founded in 1889 as a direct and somewhat more respectable offshoot of the Guild of St. Matthew. The founders were all Oxford men, all clerics, all academically inclined, and many of them were also aristocrats who succeeded to the episcopacy. They, too, were touched by the Maurician influence as well as by the idealism that pervaded academic circles in late nineteenth-century England. Much of this idealism flowed into the socialist movements through the Oxford philosopher T. H. Green. This was particularly true with regard to the principal leaders of the Christian Social Union, Charles Gore and Scott Holland. From Green they learned to think of the state as a moral organism.

Green's influence was enormous. R. G. Collingwood wrote of him:

> The school of Green sent out into public life a stream of ex-pupils who carried with them the conviction that philosophy, and in particular the philosophy they had learned at Oxford, was an important thing, and that their vocation was to put it into practice. This conviction was common to politicians as diverse in their creeds as Asquith and Milner, churchmen like Gore and Scott Holland, social reformers

---

[17] Headlam, quoted in F. G. Bettany, *Stewart Headlam: A Biography* (London: John Murray, 1926), p. 132.

[18] Ibid., p. 129.

[19] Jones, *Christian Socialist Revival,* p. 164.

like Arnold Toynbee, and a host of other public men whose names it would be too tedious to repeat. Through this effect on the minds of its pupils, the philosophy of Green's school might be found, from about 1880 to about 1910, penetrating and fertilizing every part of the national life.[20]

Green's philosophy of freedom was especially attractive to his young students. Since the human personality is basically social, he wrote, freedom "is the maximum of power for all members of human society alike to make the best of themselves."[21] Freedom was not the preserve of the privileged few; it could not be bought at the price of slavery. As the greatest of blessings, it must be equally developed in all. Freedom thus defined is the goal of social action, a property of man conceived not merely as an individual but as a person situated in a complex web of social relations. In the same article Green deplored the state of the working class and urged state legislation on their behalf as a protection against the excesses of capitalism.

Brooke Foss Westcott was the first president of the Christian Social Union. He too had studied under Maurice at Cambridge and echoed the current idealism by stressing organicism over individualism and by opposing competition in the name of cooperation. Westcott had a passion for unity and noted in a speech in 1896 that "through all the changes of the last fifty years one general influence has everywhere made itself felt; the growing sense of the interdependence, the continuity, and the solidarity of all finite things."[22]

Westcott spoke to a church congress in 1890 on the subject of socialism. The speech, later widely circulated as a pamphlet, contains an exceptionally clear statement of what the Christian socialists understood by the term socialism. It is worth quoting at length:

> The term Socialism has been discredited by its connection with many extravagant and revolutionary schemes, but it is a term which needs to be claimed for nobler uses. It has no necessary affinity with any forms of violence, or confiscation, or class selfishness, or financial arrangement. I shall therefore employ it apart from its historical associations as describing a theory of life, and not only a theory of economics. In this sense Socialism is the opposite of Individualism, and it is by contrast with Individualism that the true character of Socialism can best be discerned. Individualism

[20] R. G. Collingwood, quoted in Frederic A. Iremonger, *William Temple* (London: Oxford University Press, 1948), p. 39.

[21] Thomas H. Green, "Freedom and the Common Good," in Lloyd D. Easton, ed., *Ethics, Policy and Social Ends* (Dubuque, Iowa: Wm. C. Brown Company, 1955), p. 231.

[22] Alex R. Vidler, *F. D. Maurice and Company* (London: SCM Press, 1966), p. 272.

14

and Socialism correspond with opposite views of humanity. Individualism regards humanity as made up of disconnected or warring atoms; Socialism regards it as an organic whole, a vital unity formed by the combination of contributory members mutually interdependent. It follows that Socialism differs from Individualism both in method and in aim. The method of Socialism is co-operation, the method of Individualism is competition. The one regards man as working with man for a common end, the other regards man as working against man for private gain. The aim of Socialism is the fulfillment of service, the aim of Individualism is the attainment of some personal advantage, riches, or place, or fame. Socialism seeks such an organization of life as shall secure for everyone the most complete development of his powers; Individualism seeks primarily the satisfaction of the particular wants of each one in the hope that the pursuit of private interest will in the end secure public welfare."[23]

The stated aims of the CSU were: (1) to claim for the Christian Law the ultimate authority to rule social practice; (2) to study in common how to apply the moral truths and principles of Christianity to the social and economic difficulties of the present time; and (3) to present Christ in practical life as the living master and king, the enemy of wrong and selfishness, and to show the power of righteousness and love. In explaining these aims, Scott Holland declared that two "deep convictions" should motivate Christians involved in social action: "First, the present situation is intolerable, and second its solution must be found in the unfaltering assertion of moral, as supreme over mechanical, laws."[24] And he wrote in 1911: "Socialism in emphasizing the moral significance of the state has got hold of the real trend of things, under which we are all mentally and rationally moving."[25]

In a lecture in 1891 Charles Gore was similarly concerned with the moral problem.

What I am complaining of, what I want you to complain of, with a persistence and a conviction which shall make our complaint fruitful of reform, is—not that commercial and social selfishness exists in the world, or even that it appears to dominate in society, but that its profound antagonism to the spirit of Christ is not recognized, that there is not amongst

[23] Brooke Foss Westcott, quoted in Binyon, *Christian Socialist Movement*, pp. 162–63.

[24] Scott Holland, quoted in Jones, *Christian Socialist Revival*, p. 79.

[25] Scott Holland, quoted in Maurice B. Reckitt, *Maurice to Temple: A Century of the Social Movement in the Church of England* (London: Faber & Faber, 1947), p. 153.

us anything that can be called an adequate conception of what morality means.[26]

And to the Pan-Anglican Conference of 1908, Gore issued this strong statement:

> We must identify ourselves with the great impeachment of our present industrial system. We must refuse to acquiesce in it. But more than this, we must identify ourselves, because we are Christians, with the positive ethical ideal of Socialist thought. . . . The socialistic movement is based upon a great demand for justice in human life. . . . The indictment of our present social organization is indeed overwhelming. And with the indictment Christianity ought to have the profoundest sympathy. *It is substantially the indictment of the prophets.*[27]

Of his coreligionists Westcott demanded a change of heart and called not only for social action but for penance as well (a frequent note in the utterances of the Christian socialists).

The Christian Social Union had been founded chiefly as a study group for the self-education of Anglican clergymen, and their publications, particularly the important series of essays *Lux Mundi* in 1889, were their major accomplishment. But their approach combined theory with social activism. They agitated on behalf of a variety of social causes, including opposition to the Boer War and secular education (which drew Gore and Headlam into open conflict). Westcott was involved as a mediator in a coal strike in 1892. The union succeeded notably in its stated aim of reshaping the conscience of the church. The Pan-Anglican Conference of 1908 was the high-water mark for their cause. That so many of their members, such as Gore and Westcott, became bishops was another index of their impact.

Good Friends and Gay Companions

The Church Socialist League, the last of the socialist groups to be considered here, was organized in 1906. That was the year of the establishment of the Labour party and a general election which sent fifty-three members from the new party to the House of Commons. The league grew out of a religious community Charles Gore had founded in the north of England, though it had many affinities with Headlam's Guild of St. Matthew (overlapping membership was common among the Christian socialist organizations). The Reverend

---

[26] Charles Gore, quoted in John Lewis, Karl Polanyi, and D. K. Kitchin, eds., *Christianity and the Social Revolution* (London: Victor Gollancz, 1935), p. 192.
[27] Ibid.

Frederick Lewis Donaldson gave the Church Socialist League its motto: Christianity is the religion of which socialism is the practice. The league was more prolabor than had been its predecessors, more politically active, and more radical in calling for common ownership of the means of production. One of its members, Father Paul Bull, took up a theme introduced by Headlam and Thomas Hancock in the 1880s by laying blame for the competitive spirit in society on the Protestant Reformation. Protestants, he pointed out, emphasize the individual. Catholics (that is, Anglicans), on the other hand, value the corporate life of the church. The league's statement of aims puts special stress on the collectivist strand in socialism:

> The Church Socialist League consists of Church people who accept the principles of socialism, viz.: The political, economic and social emancipation of the whole people, men and women, by the establishment of a democratic commonwealth in which the community shall own the land and capital collectively and use them for the good of all.[28]

Algernon West, in his first presidential address, described the spirit of the league:

> To us society is one organic whole; underlying all differences of class, race and language there is the unity of the race, the solidarity of mankind. This unity is a fact revealed by Christ and confirmed by science and history. . . . This unity of life and thought constantly finds expression in the close relation between theological thought and political and social conditions. . . . Christianity has never been altogether, and never can be, separated from the political conditions of the age. . . . There is action and reaction of the political and social conditions of the age upon Christianity. It is this fact which has brought our League into existence. The theory of society that harmonises most with the Christian view of the solidarity of the race and the unity of life is Socialism. We are Socialists, therefore, because our Christian philosophy leads us to recognise Socialism as a Divinely inspired thing, making for the fulfilment of the Divine Purpose for the social redemption of man.[29]

The Church Socialist League had a somewhat shorter run than most of its peer groups, peaking about 1912 (though it lingered until 1924). The distraction of World War I was one reason for its short life. Another was the appeal of the guild socialist movement to which

[28] Jones, *Christian Socialist Revival*, p. 241.
[29] Algernon West, quoted in Binyon, *Christian Socialist Movement*, pp. 191–92. One wonders where West was reading his "science and history."

many Leaguers defected. Guild socialism advocated pluralism against the collectivist idea of a single, overarching, centrally organized corporation. It owed much to the French, whose ideas of association were still percolating among the Christian socialists in England; it owed a great deal also to the revival of medieval ideas at this time. But it had many other sources. According to Peter Jones,

> The roots of Guild Socialism were implanted in English intellectual history. It drew sustenance from many sources: from the "aesthetic" anti-industrial tradition of "Tory Democracy," Carlyle, Arnold, Ruskin, and Morris; from the "Arts and Crafts" movement and the pre-Raphaelites, Burne-Jones, Rossetti, and again Morris; from Robert Owen and the socialists and cooperators of the 1830's and 1840's; from the Chartists; from the Marxians (Labor Theory of Value and surplus value); from the Maurician Christian Socialists of the 1850's. More than a trace of French syndicalism and American industrial unionism was also evident in Guild Socialism, though the movement was peculiarly English.[30]

John Neville Figgis, a member of Gore's community, was a leading spokesman for the guild notion of pluralism. The real question of our day, he wrote, "is the freedom of smaller unions to live within the whole."[31] The great historical battles for freedom, he went on, have not been between the state and the individual but between the state and various groups. The locus of freedom for Figgis was to be found in voluntary association in communities. Individual freedom is always a result of group struggle against resisting state authority. This went against a revered thesis of most socialists that the growth of freedom in history is the outcome of the benign workings of a centrist and sovereign state. It also counters T. H. Green's notion of the state as a moral organism. For Figgis, the state, far from being an agent of freedom, was rather an obstacle to the freedom that rightfully inheres in local communities, such as churches and families.

Other important writers on guild socialism were Arthur Penty, S. G. Hobson, Maurice Reckitt, Douglas Cole, and R. H. Tawney. Penty was an expert on Gothic architecture and a technophobe with a wholly glamorized view of the Middle Ages. Hobson advocated worker control through greater trade union autonomy. With Reckitt, he took up cudgels against the Labour party and urged the Fabians to disassociate themselves from it because, as he put it, with more than a touch of vitriol, "not an idea of the slightest vitality has sprung

[30] Jones, *Christian Socialist Revival*, p. 276.
[31] Quoted in ibid., p. 277.

18

from it, its literature is the most appalling nonsense, its members live on Dead Sea Fruit."[32] When the Fabians refused to vote with Hobson he resigned from the Society. For Reckitt, guild socialism offered

> the craftman's challenge and the blazing democracy of William Morris; the warning of Mr. Belloc against the huge shadow of the servile state, and perhaps, something also of his claim of the individual's control over property; the insistence of Mr. Penty on the evils of industrialism and its large scale organization. . . . Something of French syndicalism, with its championship of the producer, something of American industrial unionism, with its clear vision of the need of industrial organization; and something of Marxian socialism, with its unsparing analysis of the wage-system by which capitalism exalts itself and enslaves the mass of men.[33]

A delightful footnote to this chapter of Christian socialism is provided by an uproarious debate between G. K. Chesterton, Hilaire Belloc, Shaw, and H. G. Wells in the pages of *The New Age*, the organ of guild socialism. Belloc argued for distributism and was sharply critical of collectivism in his *Servile State*. Chesterton had been strongly drawn to socialism as a young man and was a member of both the Guild of St. Matthew and the Christian Social Union. He became a socialist, he said, because it was intolerable not to be one. Christianity and socialism coincided on four basic points: both share a deep emotion of compassion for the unfortunate; both blame the evils of society on the competitive desire for riches; both suggest as a remedy a society based on cooperation; and both sustain a vision of a better state of affairs. Collectivism is not an intellectual fad, wrote Chesterton,

> but a passionate protest and aspiration: it arises as a secret of the heart, a dream of the injured feeling, long before it shapes itself as a definite program at all. The intellectual philosophies ally themselves with success and preach competition, but the human heart allies itself with misfortune and suggests communism.[34]

Even in the enthusiasm of youth, Chesterton did spot one significant difference between Christianity and socialism: the latter is bent upon the reformation of society while the Christian is rather more occupied

[32] Ibid., p. 294.
[33] Ibid., p. 290.
[34] G. K. Chesterton, quoted in Maisie Ward, *Gilbert Keith Chesterton* (New York: Sheed and Ward, 1943), pp. 76–77.

with reforming himself. Chesterton was from the beginning a reluctant socialist, as he admitted in his *Autobiography*. He was attracted to socialism more for what it was against than for what it was for. But he recalled the Christian socialists themselves as "good friends and very gay companions."[35] He knew Gore but was closer to Headlam and to Holland, whom he called "a man of great clearness and great fairness of mind with a natural surge of laughter within him."[36] Two other good friends of his in the Christian Social Union were Conrad Noel, whom Chesterton credits with first interesting him in Christianity, and Percy Deamer.

The Church Socialist League could not withstand the lure of guild socialism. In 1923 most of the league's remaining members, led by Maurice Reckitt and Percy Widdrington, formed the League of the Kingdom of God. The Christian Socialist League was the last of the major Christian socialist revival movements.

There were, of course, dozens of others representing virtually every denomination in England. Included in these were a number of Catholic socialist movements. Cardinal Manning deserves special mention in this context. He was far in advance of most of his compeers in social thinking. He defended the dock workers in the strike of 1889. During a labor demonstration in 1890 Manning's likeness was borne on a banner side by side with that of Karl Marx. As early as 1874 he had made an important speech on the rights and dignity of labor in which he urged state protection for workers as well as higher wages and better conditions. Labor is a social function, he said. Upon it depends human progress and the health of the state.

None of these other denominational movements, however, was as influential as the three major Anglican groups, nor were all of them together. Even so, as Reckitt recalls in his account of the period, "for all the stir they make they always remained small societies. The Guild never numbered more than 4,000; the Union, for all its moderation, had only 5,000 members when at its height in 1910; the League about the same time boasted 1,200." He adds: "When one considers not only the number of practicing church people at this period, but the wide and excited interest in social issues which characterized the years before the 1914 war, these figures appear almost microscopic."[37]

Several reasons might be given for the low numbers. One, suggested by Reckitt himself, was that all Christian socialists inherited from Maurice a distrust of systems and were therefore not keen on

---

[35] G. K. Chesterton, *Autobiography* (London: Sheed and Ward, 1936), p. 171.
[36] Ibid., p. 169.
[37] Reckitt, *Maurice to Temple*, p. 160.

planning, efficiency, and other organizational virtues. Furthermore, the Christian socialists tended toward belligerence and eccentricity; they often offended the very audience they were trying to attract. Most of the Christian socialist leaders were middle- or upper-class clergymen, a fact that created an immediate and frequently insuperable barrier to the working classes. A quip was that their message reached the bishops, but not the workers. Their background indicates another reason for their limited influence: they were on the whole more interested in theology and church reform than either economics or political reform. Finally, much of their message was more effectively carried through secular bodies like the Labour party and the Fabian Society which were much more attuned to the British temperament. Of course, many of the Christian socialists were also members of these organizations.

The Fabian Society seemed particularly congenial to them. Since its founding in 1884, it attracted large numbers of Christian socialists to its ranks. The Fabian Society was a democratic, nondoctrinaire group. Yet it was fed by all the philosophic-religious streams of the late nineteenth century, including the stream of Christian socialism. Its genius was to blend all of these influxes in a coherent and temperate fashion. Like all socialists the Fabians held to an organic theory of society (against individualism) and tended toward a collectivist interpretation of the economy. Shaw and the Webbs, for example, were critical of the guild socialists. Shaw said that if the guild premise that individual producers should pool their products were realized, then some central agency was necessary to do this effectively. Still, a wide variety of beliefs was compatible with Fabianism. It was a typically middle-class socialism whose main goal was to persuade people to become socialists regardless of their ideological bent.

Two Giants

Against this general background, we can turn to a more detailed study of the two men who have been called the greatest Christian socialists of the twentieth century: William Temple and R. H. Tawney. They were born within a year of each other, attended Rugby and Oxford together, and shared a concern with social problems until Temple's death in 1944 (Tawney lived until 1962). As Ross Terrill writes: "The mutual influence was great. Intellectually perhaps Tawney was an even greater influence upon Temple than Temple upon him, partly because Temple was more able to rummage in Tawney's field of social questions than Tawney was to tackle Temple's discipline of theology."[38] Despite important differences between the two men, it may not be stretching an analogy to regard them as the Damon and Pythias of twentieth-century Christian socialism.

William Temple was one of the young luminaries at the Pan-Anglican Conference of 1908. He came armed with a superior education—the best, in fact, that England could provide—a heart ablaze with religious zeal (he had just been ordained a deacon that year), a passion for social reform, and a not insignificant record of social involvement. At Oxford he had read the plays of Shaw and had fallen under the influence of Charles Gore, "from whom I have learnt more than from any other now living of the spirit of Christianity, and to whom more than any other . . . I owe my degree of apprehension of its truth."[39] Since Temple's father was then Archbishop of Canterbury, such praise can scarcely be considered faint.

His mentor during his undergraduate years was Edward Caird, who had succeeded T. H. Green as the foremost interpreter of idealistic philosophy. Caird's impact upon the young Temple must be reckoned at least equal to that of Gore. Caird philosophized under the direct influence of Kant and Hegel, an influence that was shaded by ancillary currents of evolutionary thought and a lifelong commitment to religious principles. His philosophy, A. K. Stout writes in a lucid summary,

> was a form of speculative idealism. It was essentially a philosophy of reconciliation. The need for philosophy, he held, arises from the apparently irreconcilable opposition between different elements of spiritual self—between subject and object, religion and science, freedom and determination, reason and desire. Unless we reconcile these antagonisms in a higher unity, we cannot achieve the spiritual harmony without which the highest achievements of man are impossible.[40]

Two marks of Temple's intellectual temperament can be traced directly to Caird's influence: the synthetic bent of his mind and his constant effort to apply theory to the practical order. In this light it is not surprising that Temple joined the Labour party in 1905 and in 1906 became president of the Workers Educational Association, a post he held until 1924. He ever afterward regarded this appointment as the signal achievement of his early years. Education served for

[38] Ross Terrill, *R. H. Tawney and His Times: Socialism as Fellowship* (Cambridge: Harvard University Press, 1973).

[39] William Temple, quoted in Iremonger, *William Temple*, p. 488.

[40] A. K. Stout, "Edward Caird," in *The Encyclopedia of Philosophy*, ed. Paul Edwards (New York: Macmillan Company, 1967), vol. 2, p. 5.

Temple, as for Maurice before him, as the middle term between the principles of religion and philosophy on the one hand and the brute problems of the social order on the other. It furnished a unique opportunity to test his abilities to bring opposing elements into harmony.

The Workers Educational Association had been founded some years before on the belief that education was the royal road to social emancipation. Tawney assessed the significance of the movement as

> a recognition by ever wider sections of the working class movement that if it is to solve its own problems, mobilize its own forces, and create a social order more in conformity with its own ideals, it must attend to the education of its members with the same deliberation and persistence which it has brought to the improvement of their economic position.[41]

Temple's thinking on the problem of worker education was pure Caird. Morality requires, he argued, the full development of the workers' powers and capacities. For Temple, the fullest expression of these powers was the basis of justice and freedom, both moral and political, and the means by which all conflict between the real and the ideal could be eliminated. Education, of course, was the instrument of such a realization. Until education so conceived has played its role the workers would be unable to set their ideals upon a firm foundation and, failing this, would not be able to have a responsible voice in their own affairs. In accents unmistakably those of Edward Caird, Temple said in a speech:

> You can have no real freedom because until a man's whole personality has developed he cannot be free in his own life; he will not be capable of forming the ideal to satisfy his whole nature, and then setting himself steadily in the pursuit of it; the further a man is from receiving the full development of his powers, the further is he from the possibility of really living his own life.[42]

Temple was also fascinated by the challenge of reconciling the traditional and modern elements of education. The traditional type, in which he had been so thoroughly immersed, relied on models from the classical past and was, largely because of this dependency, elitist and bookish. Modern education, by contrast, was rooted more in the world of experience and was more democratic and gave more importance to facts. Temple believed that the strengths of both types

[41] R. H. Tawney, quoted in Iremonger, *William Temple*, p. 75.
[42] Quoted in ibid., p. 79.

23

ought to be preserved. He saw clearly a dilemma that still plagues higher education: a traditional liberal arts education can become lifeless and merely formal for lack of contact with the empirical world, while more modern education tends to become sterile and merely vocational for want of contact with the vitalizing thought of the past. In 1912, in his presidential address to the Workers Educational Association, Temple made these remarks:·

> Now I wish to express a purely personal conviction with regard to these two types of teaching, and it is this: while we have got to incorporate all, or at any rate nearly all, that the more modern type of education has given us, it has got to be used in such a way as to leave the great marks of the traditional type predominant. Education, I hold, should remain primarily corporate rather than individual, primarily spiritual (that is, effective through influence, and through an appeal to sympathy and imagination), rather than primarily intellectual (that is, effective through an appeal to intelligence and memory), primarily concerned with giving people the power to pronounce judgment on any facts with which they may come into contact rather than supplying them simply with the facts. It should be primarily cooperative and not primarily competitive. . . . It is the traditional type that must control, because the traditional type on the whole stands for spirit against machinery. I have no doubt it is true that the old schools and universities are amateurish in method: and I have no doubt that we ought to organize ourselves more efficiently. There is a good deal of waste that may be saved: but I shall regret the day when we become efficient at the cost of our spirit.[43]

Thus the young deacon who addressed the Pan-Anglican Conference in 1908 was not just another promising cleric down from Oxford. He held views of a definite socialist cast (he was shortly to become chairman of the Christian Social Union) that had already been tested to some extent in the real world. The conference afforded him an opportunity to make the first public confession of his social philosophy, which at that time amounted to a political faith. Like all Christian socialists in the lineage of Maurice (as Temple clearly was), he construed the social problem primarily as a religious problem. He told the conference:

> This is not an economic question. It is a question touching the nature of human personality. It asks what are the deepest and most potent motives of the human soul. The question is not economic—to the Christian it is religious. . . . As

[43] Temple, "Address to the Workers Educational Association," ibid., pp. 83–84.

24

citizens we are guilty of a whole system of oppression: it is there; we tolerate it, and so become responsible for its results. There is nothing inevitable in it: it is all the result of human choices . . . and by human choices it can be modified. Here lies our duty—and our guilt.[44]

"The Church and the Labour Party: A Consideration of their Ideals," an article that Temple published in *The Economic Review* in April 1908, contains an even stronger statement of his socialist beliefs:

In the Epistle to the Ephesians, where St. Paul achieves the completion of his doctrine, he preaches the fullest scheme of evolutionary socialism, so far as all fundamental points are concerned, that has yet been conceived by man. . . . The Church is bound to recognize the justice, the essential Christianity, of the Labour Movement; the alternative is internal decay and ultimately dissolution. . . . This movement is in a deep and true sense Christian; to stand aside from it would be to incur the guilt of final and complete apostasy, of renunciation of Christ, and of blasphemy against His Holy Spirit. . . . Socialism . . . is the economic realization of the Christian Gospel. . . . The alternative stands before us—socialism or Heresy; we are involved in one or the other.[45]

Temple's life was full and unbelievably active. His rise through the ranks was stellar. In 1921 he was made bishop of Manchester and in 1929 archbishop of York, on a direct approach to the see of Canterbury, to which he was appointed in 1942. In 1934 he published his Gifford Lectures under the title *Nature, Man and God*. There he proclaimed the essential materiality of Christianity and its kinship with the Marxist understanding of history. In his preface he acknowledges that the dialectical materialism of Marx, Engels, and Lenin

has so strong an appeal to the minds of many of our contemporaries and has so strong a foundation in contemporary experience, that only a Dialectic more comprehensive in its range of apprehension and more thorough in its appreciation of the interplay of factors in the real world, can overthrow it or seriously modify it as a guide to action.[46]

Temple, of course, had learned to appreciate dialectical thinking from Caird. But in the intervening years it had become for him more

[44] Temple, quoted in ibid., pp. 95–96.
[45] Temple, quoted in *Marxism and Christianity*, ed. Herbert Aptheker (Atlantic Highlands, N.J.: Humanities Press, 1968), p. 203.
[46] Ibid., p. 204.

an instrument of apologetics, a means of making the Christian faith relevant in the social context of the times. He defended the unity of matter and spirit as the best means to secure the dominion of the latter over the former. He was not interested in dialectical materialism as such but in what he preferred to call dialectical realism. In adopting this terminology, Temple wished to agree with the Marxists that mind emerges out of matter yet acts upon its own principles and is therefore not to be identified with matter. He disagrees, however, that mind is a secondary phenomenon. On the contrary, "it is from an assertion of the reality of matter that we reach our conviction of the supremacy of spirit."[47] This is, if not quite the idealism of Caird, a much more spiritualized concept of matter than is allowable in the Marxist scheme. In the following passage Temple eloquently asserts the material character of Christianity and at the same time upholds its subordinate character. His dialectic would appear to be a somewhat uneven one: in it, the unity of mind and matter really means a relationship in which one element is superior to the other.

> It may safely be said the one ground for the hope of Christianity that it may make good its claim to be the true faith lies in the fact that it is the most avowedly materialist of all the great religions. It affords an expectation that it may be able to control the material, precisely because it does not ignore or deny it, but roundly asserts alike the reality of matter and its subordination. . . . By the very nature of its central doctrine Christianity is committed to a belief in the ultimate significance of the historical process, and in the reality of matter and its place in the divine scheme.[48]

Joseph Fletcher distinguishes three phases in Temple's ideas about socialism. The first, extreme phase was typified by his early statements at the Pan-Anglican Conference. In the second stage, represented by his Gifford lectures, Temple was using the method of dialectical thinking to further religious ends. In his first phase he favored the abolition of private property; in the second stage he had changed his mind and claimed that free enterprise might be preferable to state control. The third and last stage, says Fletcher, "was a pluralistic one, favoring the use of both principles, private and public. It was a policy under which both ownership and control could be either public or private as conditions might suggest."[49]

Temple's *Christianity and Social Order* is symptomatic of this final

[47] Ibid., p. 209.

[48] Ibid., p. 206.

[49] Joseph Fletcher, *William Temple: Twentieth-Century Christian* (New York: Seabury Press, 1963), p. 181.

period. He begins this little volume with a moderate, almost timid defense of the church's right to intervene in social matters. He offers four reasons to justify this right. The first seems unarguable: It is based on the church's sympathy for the suffering. The second reason is only partially convincing, based as it is upon the educational influence of social and economic institutions. If the latter are character-forming, then the church must have a legitimate say in determining which of their values shall count as acceptable ones. The church must see to it that the formation of character is in a Christian direction. One could not take this line of reasoning very far in a pluralistic society before encountering serious difficulties. Temple's third argument is a moral one of justice and seems shaky indeed. "Apart from faith in God," Temple writes, "there is really nothing to be said for the notion of human equality. Men do not seem equal in any respect, if we judge by available evidence."[50] The brotherhood of man is rooted in the fatherhood of God: given this religious premise, justice is necessary, according to Temple. While this argument is true, it seems to deny any natural grounds for justice, ignoring a vast body of literature that speaks directly to the point at issue. The fourth reason appeals to the natural order of things and is even more problematic. The argument is a familiar one: in creating the world, God assigned every field of human activity a purpose. It is the business of the church to monitor society to ensure that it is in conformity with the natural order determined by the Creator and, if not, to bring it back to that order. The church, says Temple, "is bound to interfere because it is by vocation the agent of God's purpose, outside the scope of which no human interest or activity can call."[51]

This is not only rather conservative theology, but it is based on one of the most conservative of all philosophical tenets: the idea of natural law. Temple devotes a whole chapter to it and makes clear his meaning of the term: "So far as reason enables us to reach the truth about anything in its relationships, it enables us to see it as it is in the mind of God. . . . As God is the Creator, this Natural Order is His Order and its law is His Law."[52] Temple acknowledged his indebtedness to Thomas Aquinas's teaching on natural law, but it seems a strange weapon (and a strange source!) to find in the hands of a professed socialist, the more so when Temple draws conclusions from it that are far from self-evident. For example, he infers from

[50] William Temple, *Christianity and Social Order* (New York: Seabury Press, 1977), p. 137.
[51] Ibid., p. 60.
[52] Ibid., p. 78.

the theory of natural law that wealth is essentially social "and therefore subject at all points to control in the interest of society as a whole."[53] The point may be valid but it would be hard to prove it from natural law.

There is an analogy here with Temple's early teaching on the nature of morality in his Gifford lectures, in which he argued that the source of moral obligation is social relationships. This is part of his argument against the individualism of such fathers of modernity as Descartes and Luther and such undesirable social attitudes as self-centeredness and assertiveness that flow from that individualism. It is also part of Temple's strategy to affirm the essence of human nature as social. This position was sharply criticized by the philosopher A. E. Taylor. For one thing, said Taylor, it exalts the state over the individual. Worse than that, it eliminates the individual as a source of moral obligation. Descartes may have gone too far in asserting the primacy of the self, but there are still good arguments that the self is primary. Furthermore, Taylor adds with a slight twist of the knife, Temple is inconsistent when he simultaneously argues that as children of God our ultimate allegiance is to Him.[54] If the source of morality is God, it would seem to be individual rather than social in nature.

The heart of *Christianity and Social Order* is a presentation of Temple's social principles. He offers as a general, guiding principle "the fullest possible development of individual personality in the widest and deepest possible fellowship."[55] Then follow the "fundamental principles," which are divided into primary and derivative. There are two primary principles: an understanding of God and his purpose; and an understanding of man in his dignity, tragedy, and destiny. The three derivative principles are freedom, fellowship, and service. Finally, Temple puts forth six practical objectives: decent housing; basic education; a secure income; a voice in the direction of the enterprise in which workers are employed; a five-day workweek with paid vacations; and the liberties of worship, speech, assembly, and association. Interestingly, Temple develops these practical proposals in an appendix.

All in all, *Christianity and Social Order* is not a radical book; in fact it is scarcely a socialist book. Its tone is one of episcopal sobriety, and its demands are moderate. We find Temple eschewing the term *socialism* because, as he explains, "socialism is a vague term. To put

[53] Ibid., p. 80.

[54] Robert Craig, *Social Concern in the Thought of William Temple* (London: Victor Gollancz, 1963), p. 137.

[55] Temple, *Christianity and Social Order*, p. 97.

it shortly, we have talked in a doctrinaire fashion about socialism and individualism long enough."[56] Then in the unmistakable voice of the great compromiser, he writes: "It is time to try to get the best out of both. The question now is not—Shall we be socialists or shall we be individualists? But—How socialist and how individualist shall we be?"[57] This is a very different Temple from the young cleric who shouted his either/or declamations at the Pan-Anglican Conference of 1908.

There are other strains of realism in *Christianity and Social Order*. For example, Temple gives self-interest a place not common in the writings of the Christian socialists, including his own earlier writings. Self-interest necessarily "plays a large part in governing society and shaping character."[58] In a judgment that might have come from Adam Smith, he says: "The art of government in fact is the art of so ordering life that self-interest prompts what justice demands."[59] There is also a greater realism in Temple's acknowledgment of the fallen, tragic character of human nature. The doctrine of Original Sin, "should make the Church intensely realistic, and conspicuously free from Utopianism."[60] He concedes that capitalism in Great Britain "has certainly given to the mass of the people a higher standard of living—a larger enjoyment of material goods—than any previous system. Moreover, it seems nearly certain that no other system would have developed so rapidly or so far the new powers conferred by modern science."[61] His stand on private property, finally, is strictly traditional: private property is lawful as an accommodation to man's sinful state.

Temple became more conservative as he grew older. Tawney, on the other hand, kept the socialist faith bright and untarnished until the end. He disliked the term Christian socialist, and from time to time doubts were expressed about the strength of his Christian commitment. Beatrice Webb used to worry that he might be no more than a religiously inclined agnostic. It is true that Tawney did not wear his religion on his sleeve and openly confessed to a dislike of theology. On one occasion he said a fitting offering to the deity might be a holocaust of theologians. But his outlook was deep formed in the same tradition as the Anglican divines. He clove the well-trodden socialist path up through the Christian Social Union and the

[56] Ibid., p. 99.
[57] Ibid., p. 95.
[58] Ibid., p. 100.
[59] Ibid., p. 65.
[60] Ibid., p. 61.
[61] Ibid., p. 81.

Workers Educational Association (with which he was associated for more than fifty years), the Fabian Society, and the Labour party. His central ideas on personhood, power, and society were derived from Christian assumptions, to which he remained remarkably faithful.

Tawney's case against industrial capitalism may be gathered from this passage in his early tract *The Acquisitive Society:*

> The burden of our civilization is not merely, as many suppose, that the product of industry is ill-distributed, or its conduct tyrannical, or its operation interrupted by embittered disagreements. It is that industry itself has come to hold a place of exclusive predominance among human interests, which no single interest, and least of all the provision of the material means of existence, is fit to occupy. Like a hypochondriac who is so absorbed in the processes of his own digestion that he goes to his grave before he has begun to live, industrialized communities neglect the very objects for which it is worthwhile to acquire riches in their feverish preoccupation with the means by which riches can be acquired.[62]

One catches no hint here that capitalism is a pluralistic system comprising economic, political, and cultural elements. There is a profound other worldliness in Tawney, a distaste for possessions and a complete indifference to goods. In an early diary entry he wrote:

> If we realized the riches that lie within everyone of us we should know that we can all afford to be spendthrift of nine-tenths of the possessions which we treasure: success, praise, and a good opinion among men, achievements, and still more material being. . . . Never be afraid of throwing away what you have. If you *can* throw it away it is not really yours. If it is really yours you cannot throw it away.[63]

No master of novices in a monastery could have put the point better!

In *The Acquisitive Society*, Tawney defined society as a community of wills devoted to common ends. He lamented the passing of a time when "the conception of men as united to each other, and of all mankind as united to God, by mutual obligations arising from their relation to a common end . . . had been the keystone holding together the social fabric."[64] Now that the keystone is gone, what remains is "private rights and private interests, the materials of a society rather than society itself, in which a mechanism of production

---

[62] R. H. Tawney, *The Acquisitive Society* (New York: Harcourt Brace, 1920), pp. 183–84.
[63] R. H. Tawney, quoted in Ross Terrill, *R. H. Tawney and His Times: Socialism as Fellowship* (Cambridge: Harvard University Press, 1973), p. 117.
[64] Tawney, *The Acquisitive Society*, p. 12.

and accumulation of wealth has become an end in itself."[65] Against the acquisitive society, Tawney postulates a functional society in which all tendencies are subordinate to common ends. The concept of a functional society is central in his social philosophy. In such a society all rights and power are conditional and derivative from the purpose of the society as a whole. "If society is to be healthy, men must regard themselves, not primarily as owners of rights, but as trustees for functions and the instruments of social purpose."[66]

In this scheme industry has its place as a means to an end; private property can be justified if it is for service and stewardship. Functionless property, on the other hand, is an abomination in Tawney's eyes. Another way of putting this is to say that property serves a function when it contributes to the growth of human personality and fosters human creativity. Ownership, for Tawney, was not the key issue with respect to property. He did not agree with the collectivist views of the Fabians on this matter. Collective ownership could be as tyrannical as private ownership. Nor did he agree with the syndicalism of the guild socialists, which also could encourage self-centeredness. It is the use of property that is paramount for Tawney. The question is always: What social purpose does it serve? Ross Terrill states his position succinctly: "Tawney's idea of function meant, first, social purpose, and second, service performed in furthering social purpose."[67]

The notion of common ends, in spite of all he wrote about it, is not very clear in Tawney. Questions about it always arise: Who determines these ends? How do they square with pluralism? Can ends be shared yet not common? Common ends, in Tawney's writings, can mean anything from a shared religious purpose to a sense of fellowship. He makes this disparaging remark about happiness as the purpose of social organization:

> But to say that the end of social institutions is happiness, is to say that they have no common end at all. For happiness is individual, and to make happiness the object of society is to resolve society itself into the ambitions of numberless individuals, each directed towards the attainment of some personal purpose.[68]

Freedom, on the other hand, was an admissible social goal. But, one hastens to ask, isn't freedom as personal as happiness? There

[65] Ibid., pp. 12–13.
[66] Ibid., p. 51.
[67] Terrill, *R. H. Tawney*, pp. 171–72.
[68] Tawney, *The Acquisitive Society*, p. 29.

31

seems to be some serious muddle here, about which Terrill makes an appropriate critical comment:

> Only in the special conditions of war could Tawney's idea of common ends be valid and consistent with the rest of his democratic socialist position. Agreement on common ends is not necessary to cooperation, or to equality, citizenship, or fellowship. It could be inimical to dispersion of power. "Social purposes"—understood as a plurality of shifting purposes, democratically arrived at—was a valid part of Tawney's socialism, taking its place alongside his general Christian anthropology, democratic theory, and liberal and egalitarian values; but not common ends.[69]

A question might also be raised about Tawney's understanding of the nature of wealth. He rests a good part of his thesis on rather simplistic distinctions between mechanical and organic, functional and acquisitive, and such. It is not clear what "functionless property" would be—surely all property serves some function. One of his major points is that capitalism encourages the wrong instincts in people and militates against the ideals of service and solidarity. It could be argued, however, that, far from encouraging the wrong instincts, capitalism channels our lower appetites to higher ends, and that, far from being incompatible with service and fellowship, capitalism makes these possible.

Another of Tawney's favorite arguments is that the accumulation of wealth has become an end rather than a means, divorced from all moral restraints. From its conception, however, capitalism was wrapped in the swaddling clothes of moral theory: economics sprung from moral philosophy. Bacon set the course for the modern development when he spoke of "the relief of man's estate." The point Tawney seems to have missed is that capitalism did not so much abolish an old moral order as usher in a new one. He spends little time analyzing the strengths of capitalism as a moral force. What is also missing in Tawney—and in virtually all of the socialists under consideration—is an appreciation of technology as a powerful social force by means of which human energies were released and experience shaped in new ways. On the positive side, capitalism was one of the dynamic forms modern technology took. Since I propose to say more about this point in my final section, it need not be elaborated further here.

Tawney's *Religion and the Rise of Capitalism* originated as the first Scott Holland Memorial Lecture in 1922 and was dedicated to Charles Gore. The epigraph is a revealing statement from Bishop Berkeley:

[69] Terrill, *R. H. Tawney*, p. 217.

32

"Whatever the world thinks, he who hath not much meditated upon God, the human mind, and the *summum bonum*, may possibly make a thriving earthworm, but will most indubitably make a sorry patriot and a sorry statesman."[70] *Religion and the Rise of Capitalism* is much superior to *The Acquisitive Society*. It is well written, thoroughly researched, and sparkles with wit and eloquence. The reader is struck in the first chapter by Tawney's evocation of the medieval ideal: the great chains of being linking all human activity in a hierarchical, organic whole. Here "all activities fall within a single system, because all, though with different degrees of immediateness, are related to a single end, and derive their significance from it."[71] The first trait of the Middle Ages is the central place of religion in human life. From this follows two others: the functional view of society, and well worked out doctrines of economic ethics. "Society was interpreted, in short, not as the expression of economic self-interest, but as held together by a system of mutual, though varying obligations."[72] Economic activity (with detailed theories about "just price" and strictures against usury) was supported by the twin pillars of medieval orthodoxy: natural law, which provided an ideal standard for regulating human conduct, and a persistent ascetic strain, which viewing all things *sub specie aeternatis,* accorded low status to all commercial transactions it did not condemn out of hand. There was no question that the church was the final authority in the realm of social morality.

It might strike us as strange that a man of Tawney's talents and sophistication would hold up feudalism as a societal ideal, but it was not unusual in men of his time. Tawney is fully aware of the gap between the ideal and the reality. He grants that feudal society was repressive, static, and exploitive, in fact flawed in every way but one: it had its sights properly directed and knew the standard whence it so frequently departed. The greatest irony, of course, is that the church which upheld the standard was itself the largest and most progressive financial institution of the Middle Ages. Tawney knew all of this. He had no intention to romanticize the period, but he had to bob and weave on a high level of rhetoric to protect that intention. It is the ideal, he insists, which was important to the medievals. They took a stand "for social solidarity against the naked force of violence and oppression."[73]

[70] R. H. Tawney, *Religion and the Rise of Capitalism* (New York: Harcourt Brace, 1926).
[71] Ibid., p. 20.
[72] Ibid., p. 25.
[73] Ibid., p. 60.

Whatever emphasis may be laid—and emphasis can hardly be too strong—upon the gulf between theory and practice, the qualifications stultifying principles, and the casuistry by which the work of canonists, not less than of other lawyers, was disfigured, the endeavor to draw the most commonplace of human activities and the least tractable of human appetites within the all embracing circle of a universal system still glows through it all with a certain tarnished splendor. . . . If it is proper to insist on the prevalence of avarice and greed in high places, it is not less important to observe that men called these vices by their right names, and had not learned to persuade themselves that greed was enterprise and avarice economy.[74]

Although Tawney seems to allow for a large possibility of hypocrisy here, he is a tolerant judge. Anything can be forgiven the age because what is important in it is "the insistence that society is a spiritual organism, not an economic machine, and that economic activity, which is one subordinate element within a vast and complex unity, requires to be controlled and repressed by reference to the moral ends for which it supplies the material means."[75]

Two remarks may be made about this judgment. First, it waters the seed of painful dualisms: between spiritual and material, master and servant, machine and organism. The long tradition of incarnational theology among Christian socialists had not eliminated in Tawney (nor in Temple, for that matter) dualistic modes of thought. Second, there is a strong punitive streak in Tawney, a desire to repress and control, to eliminate even the hated enemy. In the end Tawney opts for a heroic ideal and thus succumbs to the very romanticism he would avoid. In the Middle Ages

the problem of moralizing economic life was faced and not abandoned. The experiment may have been impracticable, and almost from the first it was discredited by the notorious corruption of ecclesiastical authorities, who preached renunciation and gave a lesson in greed. But it had in it something of the heroic, and to ignore the nobility of the conception is not less absurd than to idealize its practical results.[76]

Perhaps, but this view sets a rather high premium on ideals. The critical question that must be asked here is: Of what value are ideals that are impracticable? Why cherish ideals that have so slight a prospect for realization? This point has particular urgency with

[74] Ibid., pp. 60–61.
[75] Ibid., p. 62.
[76] Ibid.

regard to the matter of common ends, to which Tawney returns at the end of *Religion and the Rise of Capitalism*. He concludes that religion has been replaced by economic expediency; the keystone holding together the social edifice has crumbled; man has degenerated from a spiritual being to an economic animal. Dark dualisms abound in the closing pages of the book! This transformation of the social order has set a new question: To what ends is the new economic power to be subjected? Tawney writes:

> To convert efficiency from an instrument into a primary object is to destroy efficiency itself. For the condition of effective action in a complex civilization is cooperation. And the condition of cooperation is agreement, both as to the ends to which effort should be applied, and the criteria by which its success is to be judged. Agreement as to ends implies the acceptance of a standard of values, by which the position to be assigned to different objects may be determined.[77]

The singular merit of the Christian church was to have furnished such a standard and sought such agreement; it asserted "the superiority of moral principles over economic appetites."[78] Men are to be judged, says Tawney, "by their reach as well as their grasp—by the ends at which they aim as well as by the success with which they attain them."[79] This is true enough, but a standard that is habitually violated is inherently flawed in the same way that unenforceable law is no law at all. The fact is that the theory of common ends worked only imperfectly in the Middle Ages. How can it be expected to work at all in the modern age? To this question Tawney provides no adequate answer.

Tawney is at once a moralist and an economic historian. Both Tawneys are much in evidence throughout *Religion and the Rise of Capitalism*, and more often than not the moralist leads the historian. Tawney believed that Puritanism was above all a moral revolution that rose majestically to the challenge of nascent capitalism. It was, he says, the first religion "to applaud the economic virtues."[80] After this breakthrough the accumulation of riches was no longer morally suspect, though the Puritans exerted great efforts to guard against the abuses of wealth. Self-discipline and social service were most frequently insisted upon as checks on the fierce human temptation

[77] Ibid., p. 283.
[78] Ibid., p. 285.
[79] Ibid.
[80] Ibid., p. 105.

to avarice. The great genius of Calvin was to see the salvific possibilities of wealth: thus, he placed his followers on the side of the future. The ancient quarrel between the Christian virtues and the economic virtues was healed by a new moral casuistry. There had not been a greater revolution within Christianity since Constantine. Luther's reform by comparison was conservative and backward-looking. Calvin did for the bourgeoisie of the sixteenth century, Tawney remarks, what Marx did for the proletariat in the nineteenth century. The role of predestination in the one was comparable to historical materialism in the other. The outcome in both cases was a fresh release of human energies and a new social design.

Puritanism was, then, a moral movement that sought the glory of God through emphasis on a disciplined life and a sanctified society. Hand in hand with the individual virtues went the effort to give Christian character a correlative expression in social institutions. Writes Tawney: "Both an intense individualism and a rigorous Christian Socialism could be deduced from Calvin's doctrine."[81] Tawney admits that Puritanism made great contributions to political freedom and social progress. Indeed, he allows that democracy, understood as "spiritual independence," probably owes more to the Puritan tradition than to any other source. It seems peculiar that Tawney does not recognize those same democratic elements in the industrial order that descends so directly from Puritanism. The delicate dialectic of self and society works most often, he asserts, in the direction of the self. But he provides no real evidence for this. One senses that Tawney simply does not like Puritanism or the economic order associated with it, even though he reserves some intellectual praise for it.

Two judgments Tawney renders toward the end of *Religion and the Rise of Capitalism* make clear his aversion. "Few tricks of the unsophisticated intellect are more curious than the naive psychology of the business man, who ascribes his achievements to his own unaided efforts, in bland unconsciousness of a social order without whose continuous support and vigilant protection he would be as a lamb bleating in the desert."[82] Note the ad hominem nature of the statement. Again, Tawney curiously undermines his own strong stand on individualism when he tells us that the distinctive note of Puritan teaching was "individual responsibility, not social obligation. Training its pupils to the mastery of others through the mastery of self, it prized as a crown of glory the qualities which arm the spiritual athlete for his solitary contest with a hostile world, and dismissed

[81] Ibid., p. 113.
[82] Ibid., p. 266.

concern with the social order as the prop of weaklings and the Capua of the soul."[83]

Tawney cannot seem to make up his mind on the question. On the face of it, the historical record, including evidence adduced by Tawney himself, would appear to invalidate the kind of disjunction between individualism and social obligation he poses. But we are not confronted here so much with an empirical matter as an emotional attitude. *Religion and the Rise of Capitalism* is a book with a thesis. Tawney holds views independently of supporting evidence. That is why his magnificent book is flawed by a certain arbitrariness and emotional intensity. Tawney beats hard on the autonomy thesis but exaggerates many of his claims. On his own argument, the social edifice is still held together by a religious perception, individualism flourishes in a social context, and the economic order itself an expression of a moral vision.

This overview of Christian socialism in England will conclude with a passing consideration of Canon V. A. Demant's *Religion and the Decline of Capitalism*. It also originated as the Holland Lectures (1949) and the title is a deliberate evocation of Tawney's lectures of some quarter of a century earlier. Demant, like Tawney, was a member of the Christendom Group, loosely associated descendant of the Christian Social Union which attracted Anglicans concerned with Christianizing the social order (including T. S. Eliot at one time). There are, says Demant, four principal reasons for the decline of capitalism: "The hostility it has brought on against itself; the break-up of its own institutional framework; its parasitism on the non-economic foundations of society; and the dissipation of the dispositions which reared and sustained it."[84]

The last two seem to him the most significant. Demant explains that the aims of the liberal-capitalistic society were taken over from a previous society but the sustaining axioms were abandoned for new ones. That is to say, "that the capitalist phase of the liberal age presupposed the social structures inherited from the ancient and medieval world; that it counted on the solidarities and dispositions thus inherited as if these would always be there. . . . On top of the organic, civic, domestic, and craft society was reared the tremendous superstructure of economic enterprise, political democracy, intellectual exploration and technical master of natural forces."[85] By aims in this context Demant means "the views men have of the good

[83] Ibid., p. 272.
[84] V. A. Demant, *Religion and the Decline of Capitalism* (New York: Charles Scribner's Sons, 1952), p. 31.
[85] Ibid., pp. 60–61.

life," while axioms refer to the justifying philosophies men hold about the nature of things. More concretely, this means that liberalism substituted a secular for a sacral outlook, immanentism for a transcendental ontology. Man is now seen only as "a drop in becoming; he has no roots in being, behind and above."[86] Thus the reason for the decline of capitalism was not so much its aims as its philosophy of existence. This disjunction brought about a variety of maladjustments in capitalism.

For example, Demant takes up a theme developed by Joseph Schumpeter: capitalism robs citizens of "an emotional attachment to the social order"; it produces alienation; it stimulates appetites it cannot satisfy, and so forth. Demant adopts Tawney's language to speak of "status starvation" and "functionless work." Again, like Tawney, Demant is no collectivist. The state is no better than raw capitalism. Men turn to the state to satisfy their "associative natures" when capitalism fails them, but the state is a false god as well. "Neither is the principle of social healing," writes Demant, that "must take place on a sub-economic and sub-political level. . . . When the state principle is invoked as a remedy for the sickness of a society overweighted by market and contract relationships, then the real disorder is more effectively concealed."[87]

The real disorder, we might suspect, is spiritual. Demant calls us back to another time when there was "a network of native communal bonds of various kinds at the basis of civic society."[88] In one amazing statement, he avers that however "ground down" men may have been before (presumably in medieval society), they could see with their own eyes "that their labour and exploits were purposive and contributory."[89] Demant's voice is a recent one in a long line of divines who exerted great effort to infuse the new order with the living breath of faith but ended on the semipathetic note of nostalgia for an order that had passed away.

[86] Ibid., p. 70.
[87] Ibid., p. 102.
[88] Ibid., p. 104.
[89] Ibid., p. 94.

2

France

Looking back over the British experience with Christian socialism, one is impressed with Ludlow's central importance as a double mirror that absorbed the light from France then beamed it back in different directions and in different modulations. His influence extended to the Continent, to Scandinavia, and to Germany in particular.

It could be argued that socialism began long before the French Revolution, but there are sound reasons for taking 1789 as the dramatic departure point of modern socialism. It was then that the ideals of liberty, equality, and fraternity became a permanent part of the modern consciousness. Behind that event burns Rousseau's declaration that men are born free but are depraved by bad social institutions. Henceforward the thrust of reform was not individual (as had been the case in traditional Christianity) but social transformation. Class struggle has been the rallying point of the revolutionary spirit since that time. France was consequently the fount of most of the rhetoric of socialism in the nineteenth century, as well as many of the programs for action. Even Marx acknowledged his debt to French thinkers.

Socialism in France first took on a secularist hue though that secularism was often deeply tinged with religious messianism. This is apparent in many of the revolutionaries themselves and is manifest in an early pioneer of socialist thought such as Saint-Simon, who is sometimes called the father of Christian socialism. Saint-Simon was a true son of the Enlightenment. He believed in progress, the unity of the sciences, universal peace, the perfectibility of man, and so forth. He was what today would be called a technocrat rather than a socialist revolutionary, for he wanted society reorganized with bankers and engineers in positions of leadership. Thus one could, as George Lichtheim does, question whether Saint-Simon was a socialist at all "even though he anticipated most of the themes destined to achieve prominence in socialist literature from the 1930s onward. He is in this sense a transitional figure, and in speaking of Saint-Simonism one is really referring to a doctrine or a set of attitudes which his disciples . . . worked out after the master had left the scene."[1] Saint-Simon's final work was entitled *The New Christianity* (1825), in which he offered a blueprint for a secularized church. His new Christianity, Douglas Cole explains, "was to be embodied in a Church controlling education and framing the code of social conduct and belief on the basis of a lively faith in God as the supreme law giver of the universe."[2] It was a secular religion, but a religion nonetheless.

This peculiar mix of religion and secularism is present to some degree in most of the early French socialists. Joseph Buchez, who with Louis Blanc developed the *associations ouvrières* which Ludlow introduced into England, based his notion of voluntary action on Christian principles of brotherhood. August Blanqui, a pupil of the bloodstained Philippe Buonarroti, wrote in 1852 that many problems of political economy, such as the equitable distribution of wealth, could be solved only in a religious context. Auguste Comte, Saint-Simon's friend and secretary, felt that a sense of religious sacrifice was necessary to save society. Pierre Joseph Proudhon assigned the clergy the duty of arousing "dormant spirits" to social awareness. He thought that if socialism took on a religious dimension it would catch on much more quickly among the masses. There was no doubt little more than expediency in many such appeals. After all, Proudhon not only was a lifelong opponent of the church but also objected to the secular religion of the Saint-Simonians, as well as to Comte's

[1] George Lichtheim, *The Origins of Socialism* (New York: Praeger, 1969), p. 39. Lichtheim adds this note:

> In French literature the term *socialisme* made its first known appearance in print on February 13, 1832, in the Saint-Simonian periodical *Le Globe*, then edited by Pierre Leroux. Some years earlier, in November 1827, the *Co-operative Magazine*, founded by Robert Owen's followers in England, had already employed the word "socialist" to designate adherence to Owen's doctrine. The latter implied that industrial wealth should be owned not individually but in common, on a cooperative basis, and those who held this view were styled "Communionists" or "Socialists" by the *Co-operative Magazine*. While it is uncertain whether the term originated in France or in England, early English socialism was generally impregnated with French notions. It is worth observing that Saint-Simon's French followers in the 1830s were more concerned with collective regulation of industry than with cooperative ownership of wealth: there was thus from the start an ambiguity in the use of the term (p. 219).

[2] G. D. H. Cole, *Socialist Thought: The Forerunners 1789–1850* (London: Macmillan, 1953), p. 44.

"religion of humanity." Like Robert Owen, he thought religions of all kinds interjected a principle of authority that prevented the people from making their own decisions and controlling their own destinies.

The test case for religious socialism in early nineteenth-century France was Robert Lamennais (1782–1854), another of those colorful eccentrics who enliven the history of the movement. Ludlow was impressed with the group of liberal Catholics Lamennais had gathered around him, including the influential journalist Louis Veuillot; Henri Lacordaire, who collaborated on *L'Avenir* and later edited *L'Ere nouvelle*, which advocated an alliance of Christianity and democracy; Armand de Melun, one of the first Catholics to become involved in the organization of charities and founder of Le Comité des Oeuvres in 1842 and later the Société Internationale de Charité; Villeneuve-Bargemont, who as a high administrative official was able to facilitate social legislation; Frédéric Ozanam, an editor with Lacordaire on *L'Ere nouvelle* and the founder of the St. Vincent de Paul Society ("God does not make paupers," Ozanam declared, "men do"); Charles de Coux, who claimed that Catholicism offered the basis for the most admirable social economy the world has ever known; and the Comte de Montalembert, coeditor of *L'Avenir*, who believed that democracy was the natural goal of political progress.

According to Parker Thomas Moon, these Catholic reformers

> may be said to have laid down at least five planks in what was to become the platform of the Social Catholic movement: (1) instinctive rebellion against the teachings of the Liberal school of political economists; (2) an appeal to Christian charity and to Christian morals as the basis of a sounder economic and social philosophy; (3) faith in labor organization, and specifically in the possibility of reconstructing or adapting the medieval guild system to meet modern needs; (4) insistence upon the justice of a minimum wage sufficient to support the workingman and his family in a style befitting human dignity and Christian decency; (5) advocacy of social legislation to protect the working classes, above all the women and children, against the ruthless pressure of modern industrial methods.[3]

In general the French Catholics had the same general aim as many in Britain: to liberalize the church in order to Christianize the liberal state and the industrial order.

Ludlow was close to some of the group and expressed admi-

---

[3] Parker Thomas Moon, *The Labor Problem and the Social Catholic Movement in France* (New York: Macmillan Company, 1921), p. 28.

ration for Lamennais himself. In a diary entry dated May 6, 1839, he wrote:

> Lamennais, that fiery reformer, carried further than he wanted to be by his own enthusiasm, willing the good, but willing it with passion, preaching it with anger, irritating some, comforting others—a man who was at once great, terrible, sublime and deplorable—Lamennais was a great genius who can be ranked with Bossuet and Luther, between Savonarola and Fenelon.[4]

Lamennais began his career as an ultramontane defender of papal claims. He was offered a red hat for his efforts but declined because by the time the offer was made his thinking was veering toward the democratic left. Quite some time before Maurice and his friends, he discerned the coming challenge to Christianity presented by democracy. Lamennais favored universal suffrage and freedom of religion as the best means to realize economic and social progress. Like other socialists he was an associationist and sympathetic to trade unionism and cooperative movements. In 1830 he began his famous journal *L'Avenir* and shortly afterward founded the General Agency for the Defense of Religious Freedom, a body not unlike the Christian Social Union.

Lamennais's influence was a major one, Michael Fogarty quite rightly observes,

> Historians vied with one another in superlatives to describe the intellectual brilliance with which Lamennais analyzed the problems of the Church in the society of his time, and the breadth and persistence of his influence. . . . The programme of *L'Avenir* anticipates in point after point that of Christian Democracy today, and particularly that strand of Christian Democracy developed in Italy from the end of the nineteenth century onwards by Father Luigi Sturzo. Lamennais defended freedom of religion, education, the press, and association, along with universal suffrage . . . and decentralization, particularly for the benefit of regional and local authorities.[5]

In a useful analogy, Fogarty points out that Lamennais stands to the development of Christian social thought in France much as Robert Owen stands to the British labor movement: each man had a major influence in general, though any specific influence is difficult

---

[4] Torben Christensen, *Origin and History of Christian Socialism 1848–54* (Copenhagen: Universitetsforlaget I Aarhus, 1962), p. 18. My translation.

[5] Michael Fogarty, *Christian Democracy in Western Europe 1820–1953* (Notre Dame, Ind.: University of Notre Dame Press, 1957), pp. 155–56.

to identify. Both men pioneered in ways of thought that were later taken for granted; both ran into difficulties with their respective constituencies; both failed to read the signs of the times in important ways.

Lamennais's approach to social problems was roundly denounced in the encyclical *Mirari vos* (1832) of Gregory XVI. He acquiesced temporarily but less than two years later published the first of what would be a number of radical books (pamphlets really) entitled *Paroles d'un croyant*. One commentator has called it

> an extraordinary book, throbbing with pity for the sufferings of the poor and with anger against the evil-doing of the powerful, and fervently calling upon the workers to join forces in order to throw off the yoke of the servitude that bears them down, and denies to them the elemental rights of men. It is clamant for the rights implicit in the equality of all men before God; and it is also deeply internationalist in spirit. Lamennais takes his stand on the universal brotherhood of men, as the basis for the equal sovereignty of the whole people—the only legitimate form of sovereignty under God.[6]

Paroles d'un croyant was Lamennais's coming out as a radical and militant social reformer. The book reflects well the socialistic spirit of the times: the dream of fraternity, the call to self-sacrifice over self-interest and competition, the dulcet tones of associationism, and, of course, a profound religious conviction that human fraternity is based upon the fatherhood of God, that the deep currents of Christianity will be the *énergie organisatrice* of the new society. The pope, not unnaturally, thought the book perverse, but it was highly popular in Europe and quickly went through some fifteen editions in several languages. A quotation or two will communicate some of the flavor of Lamennais's style.

> In passing through the earth as we all do, poor travelers of a day, I heard great groanings. I opened my eyes and my eyes saw unspeakable sufferings and woes without number. Pale, sick, faint, clothed in the garments of mourning, drenched in blood, Humanity rose before me, and I asked myself: Is that man as God has made him? And my soul was deeply moved, and this doubt filled me with anguish.[7]

And this:

[6] Cole, *Socialist Thought*, p. 192.

[7] Hugues Félicité Robert de Lamennais, *Paroles d'un croyant* (Paris: Garnier), p. 97. My translation. This volume also contains these works by Lamennais: *Le livre du peuple, Une Voix de prison, Du Passé et de l'avenir du peuple,* and *De l'Esclavage moderne.*

Do not let yourself be deceived by vain words. Many will seek to persuade you that you are free by writing the word liberty on a piece of paper and posting it in every town square. But freedom is not a poster which we read on some street corner. It is a living power we feel within and around ourselves, the guardian spirit of homes and the guarantor of social rights, and indeed the first of these rights. The oppressor who covers himself with its name is the worst of oppressors. He adds falsehood to tyranny and injustice to profanation. For the name of freedom is holy. Be on guard therefore against those who cry: freedom! freedom! but destroy it by their works.[8]

Later books were less declamatory and contained many practical suggestions for social reform. He urged, as already pointed out, universal suffrage. He made recommendations for the diffusion of wealth. He held particularly strong views on property, advocating neither the abolition of property nor the holding of all property in common. His view was that property was a function of freedom. Therefore, for everyone to be free they must first be made proprietors. This amounted to an argument that property should be more widely distributed rather than collectivized. In 1839, *De l'Esclavage moderne* [on modern slavery] appeared, a tract that anticipated Marx's *Communist Manifesto* in some remarkable ways. Lamennais argues that the capitalist-proletarian relationship is very much like the master-slave relationship of ancient times. Then, as now, slavery means destruction of the personality, dependency, lack of legal recognition. Lamennais credits Christianity with introducing the doctrine that men are fundamentally equal—in the order of nature as well as in the order of grace. Setting the empirical reality against this premise of faith, he draws the conclusion that the time has come to end slavery. Liberty must be won, he writes, for it is never conceded voluntarily. And, he avers that the workers have always led the struggles for freedom (a questionable thesis, since French revolutions were for the most part masterminded by the middle class). Lamennais did not, however, call for violent revolution. Despite his impulsive temperament, he was a gradualist in social reform, relying upon education—as did Maurice a little later—as the principal means of shaping public opinion.

Lamennais's analysis of the worker's condition in *De l'Esclavage moderne* is an interesting one and respectably analytic as well. There are, he says, three general kinds of relationships between man and society: individual, civil, and political. He then proceeds to examine

---

[8] Ibid., p. 43. My translation.

from this triple perspective the lot of peoples in modern nations (France particularly) and concludes that little real freedom exists. The first case is the easiest to make. Since the proletariat relates to society primarily in the economic order, Lamennais has only to show the disadvantaged state of the worker to carry his point. This he does by showing the various ways in which workers are dependent. He concedes that they have one advantage over the slave of antiquity: they are relatively free of physical constraints. But moral constraint is everywhere present and often "absolute." The body may not be enslaved but the will is. Thus the freedom of the workers is largely abstract because they are dependent upon the capitalist for the conditions of their livelihood. Can we say, Lamennais asks, that there is really free choice between a terrible and inevitable death and the acceptance of an imposed law? "The chains and rods of modern slavery are hunger," he concludes.[9] This is something to think about, he reminds his readers, in a country that is praised above all others for its culture, liberal spirit, and humanity. He reasons in similar fashion with regard to civil and political rights. Injustice abounds, the majority of the people are barred from political office, the ideals of the revolution are made mockery.

Lamennais was elected to the Assembly of the Second Republic after the Revolution of 1848, but he was totally unsuited for the role of organized politics. When Napoleon III came to power, his voice was effectively stilled. He spent his last years in solitude, translating Dante and drawing up a philosophical testament of his life. He died unreconciled to the faith of his fathers and was buried, as he wished, among the poor. On the day of his funeral an immense throng gathered in the streets of Paris to pay final tribute to a voice, now silent, that had once moved them deeply. Douglas Cole assesses Lamennais's significance in these words:

> Lamennais . . . was a man of immense moral fervour and of an eloquence in writing that has given his work a lasting place in French literature as well as in the history of French democracy. His thought was, from first to last, profoundly religious: he could not understand any morality that was not rooted in faith in God. He believed firmly in the certainty of human progress because he believed in God as the beneficent Creator and the father of all men. Vehemently though he denounced the evils of his time, he had no doubt, after his conversion to democracy, that it was better than any previous time in men's history; and he was sure that humanity was on the verge of an immense further advance.

[9] Ibid., p. 332.

45

This confidence, which he had been far from holding in his earlier years, was based on his belief in the unconquerable efficacy of ideas. In his own day, he saw man accepting the *idea* of human equality before God without translating it into practice; and he was certain that such a contradiction could not long endure, and that, in the conflict between idea and self-interest, the idea was destined to prevail, because God must so will.[10]

The liberal movement launched by Lamennais (and continued by his associates Lacordaire and Charles de Montalembert) made French Catholics aware of the need to reconcile traditional teachings with the direction of modern society. Francesco Nitti notes that after Lamennais French Catholics followed two different schools of social reform:

> The first treads in the footsteps of Périn and Le Play, has more or less confidence in economic liberty, limits as much as possible the intervention of the State, and does not believe in the necessity of returning to the old corporative system; the second school, instead, follows very closely the theories propounded by Hitze and Ratzinger in Germany, and by Vogelsang in Austria.[11]

Charles Périn, professor of political economy at Louvain, was perhaps the most influential French writer on social problems after Lamennais. He opposed laissez-faire doctrines and advocated limited state intervention in the economic order. Workers had to be protected against the abuses of the marketplace. Périn remained religiously conservative, opposing liberalism on the one hand and socialism on the other. The socialist movement, he thought, had split into two dangerous groups: the collectivists à la Saint-Simon and the strongly individualistic, even anarchical, followers of Proudhon. As a Catholic, Périn repudiated both extremes. In his book *Le Socialisme chrétien*, he showed a tendency, much like some of his Anglican counterparts, to transmute the social problem into a moral problem and thus weaken his concrete proposals. Nitti wryly observes: "Périn finds nothing to oppose to the ills of modern society, beyond vain formulas like 'the free Christian corporation,' 'Christian co-opera-

---

[10] Cole, *Socialist Thought*, p. 198.

[11] Francesco Saverio Nitti, *Catholic Socialism* (London: Swan Sonnenschein, 1908), p. 263. Despite its vintage, this book remains a valuable source on social Catholicism. Nitti was a leading Italian economist and was premier of Italy during World War I. His book covers developments in Germany, France, Belgium, Austria, Switzerland, England, Spain, Italy, and America.

tion,' 'Christian employers,' and many other things, all Christian, but not more efficacious simply for that reason."[12]

Rather more liberal was the thinking of Frédéric Le Play and his school. For Le Play, Christian socialism was no more than a play on words. Socialism is the enemy of Christianity, he never tired of repeating. Le Play was opposed to any interference of the state in the economic order (he was in essence a liberal in this regard); he also opposed labor organization. Le Play and Périn reacted against the excesses of the French Revolution. Both proposed as an antidote to the ills of the time a return to the Christian faith. Thus religion became the sine qua non for any possible reform of society.

In his *La Réforme sociale en France*, Le Play tells us that the two principal effects of the revolution were antagonism and instability. Society was set against itself in factional dispute and social unrest was the inevitable consequence. His program of reform is largely an appeal to traditional moral virtues (such as self-restraint, humility, a sense of duty) for which religion is the necessary guarantor. Moon is quite right when he says

> Le Play's thoroughly aristocratic version of Catholic social doctrine appealed chiefly to capitalists, to wealthy landed proprietors, to engineers—in a word, to the upper and middle classes. In Le Play's hands, Social Catholicism lost its democratic features, was reshaped on a conservative model, and was coupled up with monarchist and aristocratic ideas in the domain of political theory. Le Play, in this sense, is the successor of de Maistre and Bonald, rather than of Ozanam and Lacordaire.[13]

The French Catholics who had been influenced by the German writers were considerably less conservative. While they had doctrinal disagreements with socialists they accepted many of their economic proposals. Foremost among these was the Count Albert De Mun and the group gathered around the review *Association catholique*, which he founded. De Mun was basically a guild socialist. The energies released by capitalism were to him most immoral. He railed against usury like a medieval casuist. The French Revolution, he said, ushered in two evils: contempt for God's law and absolute liberty. As a result, society experienced greater slavery and greater inequality than ever before. The vaunted freedom of the modern age, he said, is a sham freedom; free competition is a form of warfare; the workers depend abjectly upon capitalists. Viscount de Ségur-Lamoignon,

[12] Ibid., p. 265.
[13] Moon, *The Labor Problem*, p. 61.

47

another member of the *Association catholique* group, compared the ravages of capitalism to the fall of the Roman Empire and regarded socialism as a scourge sent by Providence to bring people to their senses. The analogy to ancient times is common in the literature of the period. One Count de Roquefeul said the slavery of the modern world is comparable to that of pagan times when slaves were whipped and fettered. As the church combated that form of slavery so it must combat the same degradation in its modern form.

De Mun first became aware of the working-class problem when as a young army officer stationed in Clermont-Ferrand he joined the local Saint Vincent de Paul Society. After the Franco-Prussian War (in which he served) and the suppression of the Paris Commune (in which he assisted), De Mun, together with a fellow army officer, La Tour du Pin, organized the Association of Catholic Workingmen's Clubs, which grew rapidly. By 1875 there were some 150 of them with 18,000 members. In 1884 there were over 400 clubs with a membership of 50,000. In 1876 De Mun was elected to the French Chamber of Deputies where he was an effective and indefatigable advocate of legislation to improve the workers' condition.

In a famous debate in 1883 on trade unionism, De Mun shone. By reason of his eloquence and his deep conviction, he controlled the debate from the start. As a result of his efforts, a law was passed on March 21, 1884, which gave formal approbation to the first syndicates. He singled out the doctrines of liberal economists as the cause of the labor problem.

> Thus it has come about that not only is the individual working man isolated from his fellows, his interest being opposed to theirs, but also a grievous division has been created between those who purchase labor, that is to say, the employers, on the one side, and on the other side those who sell it, that is to say, the workingmen. . . . This social situation has received a name, it is individualism, and it is the plague which infects our diseased society, from top to bottom. An illustrious English statesman, Mr. Gladstone, has said that this century would be called the century of the workingmen. That is true if you mean that the history of this century is filled with the echoes of their sufferings and of their vain attempts to escape the yoke of individualism.[14]

Other reforms that were due to De Mun's efforts included the restriction of female and child labor by laws enacted in 1892, 1900, and 1909; accident compensation (by a law of 1898), old-age assist-

[14] Ibid., pp. 102–3.

ance (1905), old-age pension (1910), and the Sunday holiday (1906). In time the French Catholics under De Mun's leadership worked out a comprehensive program of social action. As Nitti states: "With the exception of a few points touching on religious matters, the programme of De Mun and the collaborators of the *Association catholique* is identical with that of the most advanced Socialists."[15]

From France, as is well known, the revolutionary spirit spread throughout Europe, in most cases accompanied by violence. One notable exception was Scandinavia. A possible reason for this was the combination of Protestantism and parliamentarianism in those countries. (Something similar might be said of the England of the nineteenth century.) There were, nonetheless, socialist movements there. As early as 1848, a medical student by the name of Frederik Dreier drew up a plan for an international body of small cooperatives, largely under the influence of Proudhon. In 1878 Harold Westergaard, another Dane, met Ludlow and was greatly influenced by him. This friendship, Ludlow reported, was "the most valued of my later life."[16] In 1886 Westergaard became a professor of economics at Copenhagen University and a major figure in Danish socialism. The year before Ludlow had published in *Macmillan's Magazine* the article, "The International Co-operative Movement in Scandinavia," the seeds of which had been planted many years before by young Dreier.

In the 1890s several social reforms were introduced in Denmark which impressed Ludlow. He thought in fact that Denmark was more progressive than England. He wrote this letter to Westergaard on October 6, 1905:

> I do congratulate you most heartily on being the son of such a noble little State as Denmark. England is awfully behind you. We have not dared to touch old age pensions—your pensions' scheme has been quietly at work for years. Agricultural co-operation—except to some extent in Ireland—is in its infancy. It spreads over your whole country and gives you the command, so to speak, as to butter, of the markets of the Old World. And now, whilst the sharing of profits with workers is with us, but spreading, proclaimed by only a dozen or two firms outside the co-operative sphere, your state has shared its railway profits with its workers, the mere fact of having taken into its hands some of "the

---

[15] Nitti, *Catholic Socialism*, p. 290.

[16] My information on Ludlow's Danish connection comes from Neville C. Masterman, *John Malcolm Ludlow: The Builder of Christian Socialism* (Cambridge: The University Press, 1953), pp. 243ff.

iron highways" putting it ahead of stupid lazy old England.[17]

The letter, among other things, reveals that Ludlow's concerns in old age had remained remarkably similar to those of his youth. Some years before (in 1899) Ludlow aided Westergaard in launching a journal *Vor Tid* (Old times) that for a while was the nucleus of a Danish circle of Socialists.

[17] Quoted in ibid., p. 246.

3
Germany

Socialism came later to Germany than to France or to England, partly because of its backward economic condition. The Industrial Revolution did not have much impact in Germany before 1830. Other causes of retarded social development were the lack of political unity, the absence of a coherent middle class, and Germany's dislike of France. Another reason was that a more powerful philosophical tradition existed in Germany than in other European countries. Kant, later Hegel, and many other philosophers as well, exercised a powerful influence on the German people. It might be said that the Germans were thinkers rather than doers, that they were more given to contemplation and speculation than to social reform. After Marx turned Hegel on his head, philosophy came to be a strong support of reform, but while Hegel and the other philosophers were still standing upright their influence favored political passivity and a reactionary, highly romanticized view of the state.

A final reason is worth special mention: the most active advocates of reform were for a long time in exile. Marx, of course, was foremost among these, but there were many others. Wilhelm Weitling, for example, was important, as George Lichtheim puts it, "as a representative of a kind of primitive quasi-religious communism which inevitably marked the first emergence of a workers' movement in Germany."[1] Weitling had read Lamennais and Proudhon and became famous in Europe for his political tracts. One of these was entitled the *Gospel of a Poor Sinner*, in which Christ is portrayed as an early forerunner of communism. Weitling was an intimate of Marx in Paris (although they later quarrelled), was in touch with such quasi-secret organizations as the League of Outlaws and the League

[1] George Lichtheim, *The Origins of Socialism* (New York: Praeger Publishers, 1969), p. 169.

51

of the Just, and had some contact with the Chartists and Mazzini's Young Italy group. Weitling cannot properly be considered a Christian socialist, though the religious aspect of his thought was unpalatable to hard-core socialists such as Marx.

One of the earliest Christian socialists in Germany was Franz Baader (1765–1841). He had lived for some years in Scotland and England as a student and thus learned of the impact of industrialism on society at first hand. He read the British philosophers but was much more drawn to the romantics Fichte and Schelling. Through them he was won over to the organic view of society and in 1828 founded a journal, *Eos*, to propagate his views. Baader's reaction to social problems were those of a traditionalist Catholic. He deplored the Enlightenment, the French Revolution, the British economists—indeed everything that was modern. His organic view of society did not imply egalitarianism. Quite the contrary: Community presupposes inequality, hierarchy, and a center of authority. In his ideal social order

> every part must have its prescribed or ordained place in relation to the whole, from which it follows that no part . . . may take upon itself the act of ordination. . . . This unity must come about as the result of subordinating all the parts to the unifying agency. Without an organic social hierarchy, without power, authority and subordination . . . no organism can subsist.[2]

Baader's concern for the plight of the workers was genuine. Borrowing an image common in French writings, he compared them to the slaves of ancient Greece. Only state intervention could bring about a better distribution of wealth, and Baader harkened back to the medieval theories of a just wage to ameliorate the workers' condition. Always he promoted religion as the only effective force against a mechanical, atomistic conception of society. Baader does not appear to have had much influence on his contemporaries but by 1865, as Bowen points out,

> at a time when interest in Social Catholic reform ideas was being stimulated by the literary and forensic activity of Ketteler, a second edition of Baader's *Grundsätze der Societats-philosophie* was brought out. There is good reason, therefore, to believe that Baader may have contributed appreciably to the antiliberal, antisocialist outlook of Ketteler's corporatist followers.[3]

[2] Franz Baader, quoted in Ralph H. Bowen, *German Theories of the Corporative State* (New York: McGraw-Hill, 1948), p. 48.
[3] Ibid., pp. 52–53.

Another pioneer of Christian socialism in Germany was the Lutheran Victor Huber. Huber visited England in 1844 and again in 1854. On both occasions he met Maurice and his circle. He was much taken with Ludlow's ideas on the cooperative movement. Huber's own efforts in Germany were to be along similar lines. He promoted his ideas in the journal *Janus*, which he edited from 1838 until the Revolution of 1848, and through the Association of Christian Order and Liberty, which he founded. None of Huber's efforts were very successful. In 1851 he left Berlin and his teaching post to live among workers in a small town in the Hartz mountains. Here his labors on behalf of the poor were indefatigable, though again not notably successful.

Like other Christian socialists, Huber protested the concentration of wealth in the hands of the few, the misery of the poor, and the indifference of established authorities in the church and government. He believed, as we have seen, in the associationist approach to social reform, though he was not entirely against competition. Nor did he approve extreme state intervention of the kind advocated by Ferdinand Lassalle, the founder of socialism in Germany. Of course, he took up the refrain of fraternity and Christian love. One of his schemes was a proposal for a series of colonies or "inner colonization" (as he called it). The idea owed something to some English experiments Huber observed as well as to Fourier's *phalanstères*. Each colony was to consist of some 150 units, housing four families each. Each would be self-sufficient and conducted on strict associative principles. The plan was never put into effect, however. Huber believed intensely that the working class was where the issue was joined between Christianity and democracy. While his efforts were for the most part unsuccessful, his sincerity was never questioned. When he died in 1869, he was proclaimed a friend of the people.

The major figure among the Christian socialists in Germany was the Catholic Bishop of Mainz, Wilhelm von Ketteler. Ketteler was a large, athletic man from an old noble family. He first studied law and worked as a civil servant before turning to theology. By the time he was made bishop in 1851 he was already known as a forceful spokesman for workers' rights. In reference to the socialist aspirations of his day, he said:

> I believe in the truth of those noble ideas which are moving the world now; none of them is, in my estimation too high for the attainment of mankind. I love the present age for this reason more especially, because it strives mightily for the fulfillment of those ideal aspirations. . . . Yea, I maintain in the deepest conviction of my soul, we may restore a

community of good and everlasting peace, and call into existence the most liberal political institutions.[4]

In 1864 Ketteler published his *Social Question and Christianity*, which sent shock waves through the German Church. Later Leo VIII acknowledged it as the source of some of his ideas expressed in *Rerum novarum* (1891), in which the social principles of class organization and state intervention were, within limits, approved.

Ketteler focused all of his energies on the problems of the working class. This was the social problem par excellence. The social problem, he said, is *eine Magenfrage*—a question of the stomach, or, as we might put it today, a lunch-pail issue. He drew a bead on capitalism and economic liberalism as the two main evils of the day because they dissolve the organic bonds between men. Ketteler used a vivid image to describe the state of the workers under capitalism:

> The working classes are to be reduced to atoms and then mechanically reassembled. This is the fundamental generative principle of modern political economy. This pulverization method, this chemical solution of humanity into individuals, into grains of dust equal in value, into particles which a puff of wind may scatter in all directions—this method is as false as are the suppositions on which it rests.[5]

The machine that would turn man into a machine must itself be destroyed, proclaimed Ketteler. His associationist sympathies were strengthened by a fondness for the Middle Ages, combined with a keen feeling for German *Volk* culture. Association, which he took to be a prominent feature of the medieval social system, was "a natural law of humanity" and best realized in the Germanic spirit. Association and Christianity are directly connected by the metaphor of the body.

> The body represents the most perfect union of parts bound together by the highest principle of life—by the soul. Hence we call those associations "bodies" or "corporations" which have, so to speak, a soul that holds their members together. When men combine in a Christian spirit, there subsists among them, independently of the direct object of their association, a noble bond which like a benevolent sun pours out its light and warmth all over. In a word, Christian associations are living organisms.[6]

[4] Wilhelm von Ketteler, quoted in M. Kaufmann, *Christian Socialism* (London: Kegan Paul, 1888), p. 120.

[5] Ketteler, quoted in Bowen, *German Theories*, p. 81.

[6] Ibid., p. 84.

Carrying the analogy a step further, Ketteler argued that the future of trade unionism would belong to Christianity if new organic structures could be established in the new industrial situation.

The foundation of Ketteler's political thought is to be found in his notion of freedom. Freedom—and here the bishop taps into a line of thought that had a long lineage and that flourished in German romanticism—is man's greatest prerogative, what makes him most like God. There are essentially two kinds of freedom, Ketteler taught: moral freedom and intellectual freedom. The one is a power to pursue the good, and the other a power to pursue the true. When freedom deviates from these goals it becomes deformed, a mere license. There are in every society two forces, centrifugal and centripetal. The centrifugal force propels men to form self-governing associations. The deformation of this centrifugal ideal is anarchy—the unleashing of popular passions, the setting of private interest against the common interest, the spirit of revolt. The centripetal force is political power, which has the threefold aim of protecting the rights of individuals and groups, maintaining essential services, and representing the state in international relations. The deformation of this force is despotism or some form of absolutism with excessive centralization. The political problem is therefore to strike a balance between these two tendencies. This in turn becomes the problem of curbing human egoism.

Ketteler was particularly sensitive to the abuses of centralization. This always weakens the moral fiber of society because it deprives the majority of a voice in political affairs. Liberalism was in his mind a special instance of the evil of centralization. Ketteler's analysis of liberalism carried a good deal of weight. The first trait of liberalism, he said, is to confuse equality with liberty and then, by a kind of sleight of hand, to seduce the people with liberty while pursuing only equality. The result is equality without liberty, which is another name for slavery. Ketteler did not deny certain real gains for freedom in liberalism, such as freedom of the press, but these are severely conditioned by the aims of liberalism. A second characteristic of liberalism is to heap adulation on the people. This gives the illusion that people have some power, but in effect liberalism produces only a shapeless mass, which it leads by abuse. Liberalism does not honor the principle of self-government. The third mark of liberalism that Ketteler discerned was atheism. Finally, liberalism was partial to a mechanical rather than an organismic conception of the political process. Liberalism set itself against the family, communes, guilds— indeed, all natural societies—and ended in crass individualism. The only way to reform society, said Ketteler, is from the bottom up, by reconstructing little by little each of the natural bases of the social edifice.[7]

Nevertheless, Ketteler was a gradualist and a basically conservative social reformer. He did not think, for example, that inequality would be legislated away. The poor would always be with us, no matter what social schemes were proposed. Social inequalities are rooted in nature and personality. Therefore he appealed to faith rather than to social engineering. The Christian virtues and hope for a future life were the only effective remedies for the inevitable injustices of the social order. Without religious faith, all efforts at reform will collapse for lack of a sound foundation.

After Ketteler's death his followers split quite naturally along the two seams already apparent in his own thinking. One group stressed the corporatist in Ketteler. This included Christoph Moufang, Karl Vogelsang, and, a little later, Franz Hitze. They tended to be the more radical wing, calling as they did for a reconstruction of society in functional terms—that is, society conceived as a plurality of groups yet organically united. Some of Tawney's notions of function seem to have distant roots in the thinking of German socialists.

The more conservative group followed Ketteler's meliorist policies. George Hertling was the best-known spokesman for this tendency which in time came to prevail. Hitze's *Capital and Labor*, published in 1880, "was the fullest and most extreme statement of the corporatist program."[8] It was also the last such statement. In a sustained and well-publicized debate, Hitze came round to Hertling's point of view. Bowen summarizes the controversy in these words:

> Essentially, the issue between Hitze and Hertling was whether Social Catholicism should accept or reject the existing capitalist-individualist social order. Hitze had quite frankly questioned both the moral basis and practical viability of private capitalism. . . . Hertling, while condemning many specific abuses of laissez-faire industrialism, was a firm believer in private initiative and responsibility in economic life. He was convinced that capitalistic economy operated beneficently on the whole, and he was encouraged in this belief by the example of certain humanitarian employers who under the influence of Social Catholic teachings were beginning to take an active if paternalistic interest in the welfare of their workers. In the final analysis, he thought, the faults of the existing economic system could be remedied

---

[7] See germane developments in E. de Girard, *Ketteler et la question ouvrière* (Berne: K-J. Wyss, 1896), pp. 122–46.

[8] Bowen, *German Theories*, p. 73.

by gradual processes of reform without unduly magnifying the state.[9]

In the 1890s there lived in Mainz (for a time in the house formerly occupied by Bishop von Ketteler) another important Christian socialist. This was the Jesuit Heinrich Pesch, who was born in Cologne in 1854. While in Mainz he was associated with the Center party and wrote an important two-volume work entitled *Liberalismus, Sozialismus und christliche Gesellschaftsordnung*. He stood with Vogelsang and Hitze in opposing an unregulated liberal economy. He offered instead, in the spirit of his predecessor Ketteler, a form of associationism which he called solidarism. This doctrine was to have a determining influence on *Quadragesimo anno* (1931) of Pius XI.

Solidarism emphasized the group, more particularly the "spirit" of the group, and set the welfare of the whole as the proper end of economics. Pesch makes an interesting distinction between a society that is "one" and a society that possesses "unity." Socialism, he thought, attempts to homogenize distinct elements of society into a single whole. Solidarism, on the other hand, sees unity as compatible with private property and free enterprise. Relying on self-regulating groups, it constitutes a middle ground between the ragged individualism of laissez-faire capitalism and statism. Pesch's indebtedness to Thomas Aquinas is everywhere evident in his constant effort to seek a *via media* between competing economic theories.

Pesch rejected the liberal view of society as a mere mechanism to facilitate commercial exchanges, unrestrained freedom, and an atomic conception of the individual. To this extent he favored organicism. But against socialism he argued for personal autonomy and gave a place to self-interest and competition in the economic sphere. Men have, he wrote,

> natural tasks and goals and, consequently, natural rights: the right to exist, the right to work, to acquire property, to activate their personal capabilities, the right to found a family, etc. Positive law may be concerned with the more proximate determination of the exercise of these rights. The right itself, however, precedes every positive law and cannot be suppressed by it.[10]

And he qualifies further:

> I have marked freedom as a constituent of national welfare, although not the wild freedom of arbitrariness, but the

[9] Ibid., pp. 110–11.

[10] Quoted in Richard E. Mulcahy, *The Economics of Heinrich Pesch* (New York: Henry Holt and Company, 1952), p. 164.

freedom of order. I have put down free enterprise as the rule, public enterprise as the exception. I have said: every freedom of economic trade is justified, which is consistent with the goal of the economy, with the material welfare of the people. Further than this no man can go in the demand for freedom.[11]

Solidarism bears some resemblances to the guild socialism of English socialists such as Neville Figis, although it is difficult to pinpoint direct influences. All the Christian socialists seem to have been nourished by similar ideological streams.

Some special consideration must be given here to Lujo Brentano and his role as a social reformer. Born in Frankfurt, of an old Italian family, he was trained as a liberal economist and was deeply influenced by the writings of Smith, Mill, and Ricardo. In 1867 he went to Berlin where he became interested in the cause of the working classes. His attention was drawn to England because, as he reasoned, the English had more experience with the problems of industrialization and might furnish models of social reform that had some universal validity. Brentano was, of course, familiar with the various cooperative proposals advanced during the 1860s. Such men as Lassalle, Huber, and Ketteler all favored this approach to the social problem. Brentano adopted it as well. Cooperation, he felt, would both improve the workers' lot and give them an active role in economic life. With his associate Ernst Engel, he developed a plan for "industrial partnerships." To this extent he modified but did not abandon his liberalism.

In 1868 Brentano visited England. The Reform Bill of the previous year indicated that the British were making major efforts to settle the working-class problem. The trade unions had been growing in power for some twenty years, though they were far from being universally accepted either by the leaders of business or by the general public. Brentano met Ludlow on this occasion. He had read *The Progress of the Working Class 1832–1867*, which Ludlow had written in collaboration with the old Chartist Lloyd Jones. Neville C. Masterman points out that

> Ludlow's name was for a time better known in Germany than in Britain. Besides Huber and Brentano, he came to know other Germans such as Max Hirsch, a promoter of a special kind of trade union (whom he had also advised to study trade unions rather than co-operation); Adolph Held, professor of political economy, first in Bonn, then in Berlin, an ardent State Socialist; Gustave Cohn, later professor of

[11] Ibid., p. 166.

political economy at the University of Göttingen; Walter Hasbach, author of a learned work on the British agricultural labourer; and others.[12]

For some nine months Ludlow helped Brentano study the social situation in England, particularly the trade unions. When the latter returned to Germany he proposed to Bishop Ketteler that they set up producers' cooperatives similar to those organized by the Christian socialists in England. Shortly thereafter, however, he became convinced that trade unions rather than cooperatives were the answer to labor's problems.

Ludlow proved a valuable guide to Brentano. Few knew the problems of English society as well as he did. Furthermore, he was in a position to introduce him to labor leaders all over the country. A deep friendship formed between the two and they corresponded long after Brentano returned to Germany. In his study on Brentano, James Sheehan makes this observation:

> In a number of important ways Ludlow was the perfect intermediary between Brentano and the British labor movement. Since Brentano was still a Catholic in 1868, he and Ludlow were drawn together by their common Christianity. Furthermore, Ludlow and Brentano probably shared a common psychological attitude toward the working classes, which they seem to have viewed with a mixture of fear, compassion, and responsibility. Perhaps most important, Ludlow provided Brentano with an example of a uniquely unselfish social consciousness, totally devoted to the material, moral, and intellectual betterment of the workers. In Ludlow and his associates, Brentano saw men who were actually bridging the gap between what Disraeli called the "two nations." Brentano felt they could take much of the credit for the relative tranquility of British social developments. Living in imperial Germany, where the gap between rich and poor was ominously large, Brentano never ceased to admire his achievement.[13]

Ludlow wrote of Brentano's efforts on behalf of the German working class in an article in *The Fortnightly Review* (April 1869). His article came to the attention of Karl Marx. Marx was not pleased by the manner in which Ludlow had linked his name with Lassalle, but he overlooked this in the hope that Ludlow would review the first volume of his *Das Kapital*. There were not many Englishmen, Marx

---

[12] Neville C. Masterman, *John Malcolm Ludlow: The Builder of Christian Socialism* (Cambridge: The University Press, 1963), p. 213.

[13] James J. Sheehan, *The Career of Lujo Brentano* (Chicago: University of Chicago Press, 1966), p. 29.

observed, who were both defenders of the working class and also fluent in German. Ludlow tried to oblige but found he could not get through the heavy tome. No Englishman, he declared, would ever be able to read the book. Later he reviewed Marx's *The Eighteenth Brumaire of Louis Napoleon* and had this to say about it:

> Marx is an able, laborious, sharp-witted man . . . too really learned to be merely cynical, too cynically-minded to make a favourable use of his learning; altogether a characteristic, clear-cut specimen of the German Reds, in whom righteous disbelief of the world's idols is not yet completed by belief in aught higher. . . . Marx's book is real history, full of thoughts, with all the facts ably and clearly marshalled, while the absence of favourable prejudice, whether as respects parties or individuals, gives it a position of acid impartiality.[14]

In 1872 Brentano published his two-volume magnum opus entitled *Die Arbeitergilden der Gegenwart* [the contemporary labor movement], which was based on his research in England. The book influenced the Webbs in their classic work on trade unionism and also caused Cardinal Manning to adopt a more sympathetic attitude toward the working classes. Brentano had still not entirely abandoned his liberalism, for he continued to think that trade unionism was compatible with a free economy and remained opposed to state intervention. Sheehan comments:

> Brentano felt that unions would equalize but not destroy the free market economy. . . . Thus in contrast to men like Lassalle and Marx, who sought to improve the lot of the workers by a reconstruction of the social order in which the working class absorbed the rest of society, Brentano wanted progress within the framework of the existing social structure.[15]

One of Brentano's friends and colleagues was the sociologist and economic historian Max Weber. They both belonged to the Verein für Sozialpolitik, founded in 1873 by a group of German professors interested in social action. Weber stood with Brentano in his struggles for recognition of trade unionism as well as other causes. Their

[14] John Ludlow, quoted in Masterman, *John Malcolm Ludlow*, p. 207. As far as I can determine, Marx had very little influence on the English Christian socialists and that only indirectly insofar as some of his ideas filtered through such bodies as the Social Democratic Federation or the Fabian Society. The European case is different. Marx definitely influenced figures like Ketteler and Brentano.

[15] Sheehan, *Lujo Brentano*, pp. 38–40.

friendship, however, was never an easy one and after 1912 it ceased altogether. Weber's *The Protestant Ethic and The Spirit of Capitalism* appeared in 1904-1905. Weber advanced the thesis (many years later taken up by Tawney) that the new order of capitalism was sustained by the worldly asceticism of the Protestant religions. Weber conveniently illustrates "the spirit of capitalism" with a few pages from the autobiography of Benjamin Franklin. It is an ethic, says Weber, "of earning more and more money combined with the strict avoidance of all spontaneous enjoyment of life."[16] This is not to be confused with mere greed. Greed, understood as a compulsive desire to accumulate wealth, has characterized individuals in all ages of history. The spirit of capitalism differs from greed principally in that it is a rational pursuit of wealth, buttressed by the rational organization of society. The acquisitive instincts are thus universalized through an effective control system. The distinctive mark of capitalism is "the rational organization of (formally) free labor."[17] Capitalism is thus an instance of the rationalization of society, which is the essence of modernism.

Weber does not like the new order. The prevailing tone of his book, as with Tawney, is one of pessimism and nostalgia. He speaks of the "extreme inhumanity" of the doctrine of predestination, which breeds lonely individualism and negative attitudes toward the flesh and toward the values of friendship and community, art, and work. Above all Weber laments puritanism's harsh denial of pleasure. The uncertainty of this doctrine (for how could one know that one was saved?) could in practice be offset only by "intense activity." By a strange yet rigorous logical transference, this activity came to be prized as having religious value in itself. God helps those who help themselves. Thus the Calvinists sanctioned a new range of virtues—such as industry and frugality—and thereby introduced a new technology of salvation which melded admirably with the new technology of money. Weber sees well enough that this ethic, despite certain differences, is rooted in medieval monasticism. The new asceticism is the old ascetism in a new guise. What we have in both cases is "a systematic method of rational conduct with the purpose of overcoming the *status naturae*, to free man from the power of irrational impulses. . . . This active self-control, which formed the end of the . . . rational monastic virtues everywhere, was the most important

[16] Max Weber, *The Protestant Ethic and the Spirit of Capitalism*, trans. Talcott Parsons (New York: Charles Scribner's Sons, 1958), p. 53. Franklin, of course, was more given to spontaneous enjoyments than Weber seems to have realized.
[17] Ibid., p. 21.

practical ideal of Puritanism."[18] In some deep sense, economics recapitulates theology.

It is well to bear in mind that much of religious socialism developed against the background of turbulent changes in German society. Two in particular bear noting. The first was a long, bitter, hard-fought battle between church and state, the *Kulturkampf*. From the time of Bismarck's appointment as premier of Prussia in 1862 until the end of the Franco-Prussian War in 1871, his major political efforts were bent toward unification of Germany. As chancellor of a new empire, Bismarck was understandably sensitive to anything he deemed a threat to national unity. He feared especially the centrally organized Catholic church. The *Kulturkampf* was precipitated in 1870 when Pius IX proclaimed the dogma of papal infallibility. Shortly afterward, relations with the Vatican were broken off and a series of measures were levelled against the church, including abolition of the Catholic department in the ministry of culture, state control of all schools (including seminaries), the expulsion of the Jesuits, and persecution of the clergy. Catholics rallied around the Center party and gradually carved out a position of power in the Reichstag. It was the genius of leaders like Bishop Ketteler to see the advantages of the new political situation to Catholics and Christians generally. As Fogarty puts it, they came to see that "liberal freedoms are essential for the defense of Christian interests . . . [and that] a liberal and democratic Christian party can be effective only if it is independent of the clergy."[19] Thus Ketteler was able to advance his social cause by cleverly exploiting the political situation. The Center party became instrumental in social legislation, and during the 1870s the Christian social unions grew in strength. The latter were a direct expression of Ketteler's belief in self-help organizations.

The second background development concerns the influence of technology on socialism. As the historian James Billington has shown, a new type of socialist was emerging on German soil during these years. He was an organizer rather than a prophet, a technician rather than an idealist. Structure was becoming more important than charisma. Germany was in the vanguard of the application of technology to politics. The key figure in this process was Ferdinand Lassalle, once Marx's collaborator but eventually his enemy. Revolutions failed in the past, Lassalle held, because they were too dependent on ideas. Marx's journal, the *Neue Rheinische Zeitung*, also failed for this reason. It was unable to posit an effective middle term between ideology on

[18] Ibid., pp. 118–19.
[19] Michael Fogarty, *Christian Democracy in Western Europe 1820–1953* (Notre Dame, Ind.: University of Notre Dame Press, 1957), p. 174.

the one hand and the proletariat on the other. Lassalle saw that tactical organization was the answer. At the grass roots level, both mass meetings (Lassalle was the first modern master of this medium) and a cell structure adapted to precise goals would provide such organization. This was to be complemented by party discipline and bureaucratic techniques. In 1863 Lassalle formed the All German Workers' Association (which became the Social Democratic party) on these principles.

Thus social democracy in Germany became the first socialist party to capitalize on the new technological spirit abroad in society as well as the new technological means available. Billington puts it this way:

> Social Democracy represented a systematic attempt by the Germans to convert their short-lived revolutionary confla-gration of 1848–50 into the more disciplined, slow-burning fire of a modern political machine. The German Social Dem-ocratic party sought to organize workers as rationally within society as the new engineers had organized machines inside the factory.[20]

Thus the socialist became the organization man. The Christian so-cialists in Germany (and to a considerable extent in England) were prevented by their technophobia from achieving the success of their secular counterparts—whether the Fabians in England or the Las-sallian social democrats in Germany. By the same token they doomed themselves to a position of secondary importance. On the other hand, Christian socialism avoided the terror and dehumanization that has so frequently resulted from the combination of organismic metaphors and technological resources.

[20] James H. Billington, *Fire in the Minds of Men: Origins of the Revolutionary Faith* (New York: Basic Books, 1980), p. 369.

4

Conclusion

Whatever its roots in the past, Christian socialism was an essentially modern movement. It was a response to problems that issued from the rise of capitalism and the Industrial Revolution. The primary aim of the Christian socialists was always religious rather than political, more moral than economic. They strove to uphold Christian traditions in the new economic order and to defend the faith against the atheism and secularism that often accompanied that order. They saw the abandonment of the Christian faith as the cause of the sufferings of the poor and of social upheavals. The center focus of Christian socialists was the plight of the workers under capitalism. Perhaps their greatest strength was to take a prophetic stand against very real abuses and bear Christian witness on behalf of those who were most victimized. The Christian socialists wrote prolifically and many of them had first-rate theological minds. They succeeded in uncovering long-neglected aspects of Christian social ideals and principles. Moreover, they made strenuous efforts to carry their message to the people.

This said, it must also be pointed out that they were characteristically drawn to commit what Dewey called the fallacy of selective emphasis. The Christian socialists were overwhelmingly from the middle or upper classes. Virtually all of them were intellectuals. This, of course, is the case with socialists generally. As Friedrich von Hayek has said: "Socialism has never and nowhere been at first a working-class movement. It is by no means an obvious remedy for an obvious evil which the interests of that class will necessarily demand. It is a construction of theorists, deriving from certain tendencies of abstract thought with which for a long time only the intellectuals were familiar."[1] Intellectualism is consequently a besetting weakness of so-

---

[1] Friedrich von Hayek, "The Intellectuals and Socialism," *The University of Chicago Law Review*, vol. 16, no. 3 (Spring 1949), p. 178.

cialism. It attempts to reform society downward from a plan abstractly conceived. Christian socialism was the work of theologians. They became convinced that an ideal socialism was identical with Christianity and from this conviction proceeded to specific reforms. In this they took leave of the canons of objectivity and read their own preferences into a religion that is compatible with many different political and social arrangements.

When Maurice claimed: "I seriously believe that Christianity is the only foundation of Socialism," he might have had a point. But when he added that "true socialism is the necessary result of a sound Christianity," he was selectively emphatic and weakened his case. Likewise when Buchez stated that "the human purpose of Christianity is identically the same as the revolution: it is the former that inspired the latter," he claimed too much. For this reason the Christian socialists tended to fasten on the sacramental and incarnational aspects of the tradition while downplaying the doctrines of original sin and the corrupt nature of man. Maurice, again, is typical. One of the cornerstones of his theology was a denial of eternal punishment. He would not, he proclaimed, let the fall be the basis of theology. He believed every child born into this world is already redeemed. Bishop Westcott argued that the Incarnation did not depend on the fall. Thus he preferred to preach the sweeter themes of unity and love rather than the harsher message of sacrifice and suffering. T. H. Green summed up the attitude of the Christian socialists pithily: "The sense of sin is very much an illusion. People are not as bad as they fancy themselves."[2] When Stewart Headlam was a student at Cambridge, his soul was sorely tried by the thought of hell. Maurice, as his spiritual guide, dispelled his anguish and brought him peace. In later life Headlam gave a speech to the Fabian Society in which he said: "You, ladies and gentlemen, probably do not know what it is to have been delivered in the world of thought, emotion, imagination, from the belief that a large proportion of the human race are doomed to endless misery. You are free-born—mainly through Maurice's work and courage. For myself, I say that at a great price I obtained this freedom."[3]

This theological orientation led the Christian socialists into another characteristic fallacy. Let me call it the fallacy of misplaced potentiality: they were prone either to misread or to overestimate human potential. To use Wordsworth's metaphor, they always approached the shield of humanity from the golden side. Thus they

---

[2] Thomas H. Green, quoted in F. G. Bettany, *Stewart Headlam: A Biography* (London: John Murray, 1926), p. 180.
[3] Stewart Headlam, quoted in ibid., p. 20.

often failed to evaluate truly the sluggish quality of human nature, the heavy empirical weight of habit and self-interest and convention. Thomas Paine said that we have it in our power to begin the world all over again. But we do not: we are always born into a society that is heavily sedimented with the record of human choices. Reform must always be cautiously predicated upon conditions that have been formed in the long march of history. The theology of the Christian socialists was deeply imprinted with the traces of romanticism. They stood with one foot on the threshold of the invisible world, where an imaginary land of infinite possibilities beckoned. All too often they were bewitched by the leaping fires of intuition that light up the world and make our heart dance but do not prove effective in political action.

A conspicuous instance of this tendency is the emphasis the Christian socialists placed on the communal nature of man. "Competition is put forth as the law of the universe," Maurice wrote to Kingsley in 1850. "That is a lie. The time has come for us to declare that it is a lie by word and by deed." In his *Kingdom of Christ*, Maurice expressed a vision of a New Man and a New Society in these words: "There is a fellowship larger, more irrespective of outward distinctions, more democratical, than any which you can create; but it is a fellowship of mutual love, not mutual selfishness, in which the chief of all is the servant of all."[4] Tawney spoke of a society in which we would all be "within reach of one another." The Reverend William Tuckwell, a friend and colleague of Stewart Headlam, could hold audiences enthralled as he discoursed on the Kingdom of God as utopia: "A day of wider knowledge and firmer faith, a day of equal, not of selfish aims; a day of universal brotherhood, not of class distinctions."[5] God Himself, said Scott Holland, was a socialist. All sin, declared Conrad Noel, is sin against the community. Fellowship, unity, community—these notes are a constant refrain of Christian socialism.

It is easy to be misled by such language. It stirs the soul and casts a warm glow over recalcitrant realities, but it is a deceptive language. Much of what the Christian socialists said about equality was hyperbole. Competition and fellowship cannot be facilely set over against one another. They are not incompatibles; each has a natural and necessary place in an assessment of human nature. The Christian socialists here lose sight of an important distinction in moral discourse. Man is, on the one hand, a social animal and as such

[4] Frederick D. Maurice, *Kingdom of Christ* (London: J.M. Dent, 1907), p. 336.
[5] William Tuckwell, quoted in Gilbert C. Binyon, *The Christian Socialist Movement in England* (New York: The Macmillan Company, 1931), p. 115.

pursues communal virtues; but he is also, as the poet might have said, an island unto himself. There are public and private dimensions of selfhood. If primacy is to be given to one over the other it would be wiser to favor the latter. In the end we meet ourselves, as one of Nietzsche's aphorisms has it. The appropriate distinction here is between individual and person. As individuals we share a common nature, a common situation, a common identity, but as persons we are centers of creativity, freedom, and uniqueness. This is what human subjectivity means. The Christian socialists could not free themselves in this regard of certain traditional categories of thought that emphasized the common nature of man. With Plato, they modeled man after the state (or community) and made moral worth a function of the group without seeing the totalitarian implications of that position.

This explains why the Christian socialists were fond of organismic metaphors. They quite naturally appealed to images of totality—such as community, family, church, and state—as a way of combating what they took to be the excessive individualism fostered by capitalism. The philosophical basis of Christian socialism was idealism. Maurice drew primarily from Plato among the philosophers. "I have never taken up any dialogue of Plato without getting more from it than from any book not in the Bible."[6] He was attracted by Plato's ability to subsume empirical reality to overriding principles. Beyond the puzzling facts and disorders of existence Plato postulated an ideal world as the abode of the mind. Here man dwells naturally. So Lamennais professed unshakable faith in "the unconquerable efficacy of ideas."

Facts did not interest the Christian socialists so much as ideas— the vivid mysteries shining over present realities, the unseen meanings that lurked beneath appearances. Ludlow, who professed his own kind of idealism, was nonetheless critical of Maurice's Platonism. In a sharply worded letter to him in 1852, Ludlow spoke his mind. "Dear friend," he wrote,

> Will you allow me to say that I have felt that this was one of your temptations? I have endeavored to study you very closely for the last year, both in your self and through your books (I would especially refer to the Moral and Metaphysical Philosophy) and it does seem to me that you are liable to be carried away by Platonistic dreams about an Order, and a Kingdom, and a Beauty, self-realized in their own eternity, and which so put to shame all earthly coun-

---

[6] Frederick D. Maurice, quoted in Alex R. Vidler, *F. D. Maurice and Company* (London: SCM Press, 1966), p. 34.

terparts that it becomes labour lost to attempt anything like an earthly realization of them, and all one has to do is to show them, were it only in glimpses, to others by tearing away the cobwebs of human systems that conceal them. I do not think this is Christianity.[7]

Idealism came to the Christian socialists rather directly through Hegel's philosophy and, in England, establishment philosophers like Green, who were disciples of Hegel. Whereas Platonism had supported medieval images of organism, like the mystical body and the communion of saints, Hegel's philosophy tended to generate similar images with respect to the state. Adam Ulam has shown that idealism accords a privileged role to the state as an instrument of social and economic reform.[8] It is then but a step to consider all problems essentially political in nature and to hypostasize the state. We come soon to think of the state as itself an organism, on the model of a living body that is self-directed, obeying its own laws and setting its own ends. The statism we know today drinks from the same philosophical stream.

To the degree that the Christian socialists imbibed organismic ways of thinking they were reactionary rather than progressive, harkening back to a time before the modern age when man bore an umbilical relationship to his social institutions. The great accomplishment of political thinkers like Locke and Hobbes was to free us from this kind of domination. The conception of the state they defended was not a projection of our moral selves, of "our higher self" as Hegel put it, or an organism endowed with the properties of life. It is to be thought of as a human creation for accomplishing specific human goals. Our relationship to the state is not organic but contractual; its function is to protect and preserve certain natural rights which we possess independently. In this view, there are no ends of the state apart from those of the citizens who compose it. We could not say with Hegel (in his *Philosophy of Right*) that "truth, real existence, and ethical status" can be had only as a member of the state. The Christian socialists were by no means all state interventionists, but they subscribed to the organismic view of society nonetheless. If not the state then the church was appealed to as the fundamental community. The Christian socialists in general failed to grasp that with the advent of capitalism and industry a new chapter had opened in the history of freedom. In pitting their theological strength against

---

[7] John Ludlow, quoted in Torben Christensen, *Origin and History of Christian Socialism 1848–54* (Copenhagen: Universitetsforlaget I Aarhus, 1962), p. 306.

[8] Adam B. Ulam, *Philosophical Foundations of English Socialism* (New York: Octagon Books, 1964). See especially chapter 2.

the times, they failed (precisely where they should have succeeded) to perceive the new order as a redemptive agency.

Let me make the point in another way: in opposing technology (and its principal manifestations in capitalism and industrialism), the Christian socialists misdiagnosed the most creative thrust of their age. They saw, of course, that there were problems inherent in the new order, but they interpreted these as a threat to faith rather than as an instance of God's creative work in history. In 1851 the Great Exhibition of London was held in Hyde Park. In the same year one Charles Babbage commented on the event:

> The productions of Nature, varied and numerous as they are, may each, in some future day, become the basis of extensive Manufactures, and give life, employment, and wealth to millions of human beings. But the crude treasures perpetually exposed before our eyes contain within them other and more valuable principles. All these, in their innumerable combinations, which ages of labour and research can never exhaust, may be destined to furnish, in perpetual succession, the sources of our wealth and of our happiness.[9]

Did Maurice, one wonders, attend the Great Exhibition? And what could have been his thoughts? He could not have seen, as Babbage saw, the "valuable principles" implied in that display. It did not occur to any of the Christian socialists of the time to elaborate a theology of technology, to point out linkages between wealth and spirituality, between capitalism and community, between technology and creativity. William Temple had a lot to say about the materiality of Christianity, but technology was mysteriously excluded from serious consideration. He once said: "My ignorance of all things scientific is so immense as to be distinguished."

Historically, technology antedated and made possible both democracy and capitalism, and it remains the most conspicuous feature of modern culture. Modern technology, as it began in the medieval monasteries and was philosophically articulated by such pioneers of modern thought as Descartes and Bacon, was seen as a redemptive act, an *imitatio dei*. That is to say, it was seen as a means of repairing the ravages of original sin. Two things were lost in the fall, says Bacon, innocence and power. The first is recovered by faith, the second by technology. Modern technology then is in fundamental aspects a religious phenomenon. When the Christian socialists attacked capitalism they were often in reality attacking technology. In

[9] Charles Babbage, quoted in Arnold Pacey, *The Maze of Ingenuity: Ideas and Idealism in the Development of Technology* (Cambridge, Mass.: MIT Press, 1964), pp. 293–94.

attacking technology, however, they were attacking an aspect of Christianity itself. Sweet irony! Under democratic capitalism technology has become a great force for good. Not to have seen this potential was the most serious shortcoming in the vision of the Christian socialists.

They were blinkered by their education, which was classical and humanistic, highly idealistic, and speculative in nature. They were formed for a clerical society that was fast disappearing. As a consequence, they were quite literally misfits in the new technological society, which called for different talents, different attitudes, a different mind-set. They were, so to speak, left out of the new reward system. This seems to explain their frequently rancorous attitude toward the new order. Listen, for example, to Maurice on money. "It seems to me," he wrote his son,

> as if the slow disease of money-getting and money-worship, by which we have been so long tormented, must end in death, and though I do believe inwardly and heartily in a regenerative power for Societies as well as individuals, the signs of its active presence here are not yet manifest to me. Neither in Conservatism nor Liberalism as I find them here, can I see what is to make the dead bones stir and live.[10]

This seems less a serious comment on society than a confession of his own limitations. Of all the Christian socialists here surveyed, Bishop Ketteler was the most successful as an organizer. I suspect this was due to the influence of Lassalle, who understood the new technology. The others, even the great Ludlow, wore their activism like an ill-fitting cloak, spilling out their energies in schemes that had a remarkably high degree of failure.

This conflict between the idealism of their education and the pragmatism of their circumstances produced in the more sensitive of the Christian socialists deep-seated guilt feelings. They wept copiously for the sins of church and state, but tears blind as well as cleanse. The Christian socialists lamented loudly in the industrial wastelands; they prophesied dire things to come for the children of God. Less frequently did they make cool appraisals of their situation or discern with accuracy its spiritual possibilities. Their judgment about the plight of the working classes, for example, was strangely lopsided. They were extremely sensitive to the darker sides of industrialization and had an eagle eye for human suffering. Reading

---

[10] Frederick D. Maurice, quoted in Maurice B. Reckitt, *Maurice to Temple: A Century of the Social Movement in the Church of England* (London: Faber & Faber, 1947), p. 97.

them one gets the impression that there was only a dark side. It is never acknowledged that the lot of the poor in industrial England had improved or that the standard of living rose steadily throughout the latter part of the nineteenth century, the period when the Christian socialists were most active.

Paul Johnson, in his excellent *Enemies of Society*,[11] suggests some reasons for this curious lacuna. He points out that the rise of industrialism coincided with "a new phase of human sensibility," which led many well-educated middle-class and upper-class people into the paths of social protest. On the one hand, the problems of industrial England were more visible (and for that reason often thought to be more acute); on the other hand, there was an increase in both the extent and the quality of education. The combination of these two circumstances produced a new social consciousness. Johnson also points out that many of the social ills attributed to capitalism were in fact "political mistakes." These are plausible explanations. I would not, however, want to exclude the guilt factor. The Christian socialists had a tendency to transfer to the working classes their own sense of feeling abandoned. But the latter rarely perceived their problems as the socialists did and in virtually all cases did not spontaneously accept the solutions they proposed.

One cannot ignore either in the Christian socialists what might be called, for want of a better term, the psycho-erotic dimension. Eroticism is, strictly speaking, a capacity to invest the human body with qualities of high desirability. Those in whom the erotic drive is strong easily generalize their feelings to art, the state, the church, power, or other more capacious objects of desire in order to transcend the facticity of the flesh. The Christian socialists, under the dual influence of their faith and some form of idealistic philosophy, were not naturally disposed to a sense of limits. Images of longing run through their writings; they were extraordinarily susceptible to the dramatic, the psychically charged, the spiritually exciting. They paced off the realm of the possible with giant steps. Everything is extreme today, Lamennais said; there is no longer any dwelling place in between! Modern life is characterized by boredom, in Kierkegaard's diagnosis, for which the obvious remedy is the pursuit of novelty.[12] Journalism, he thought, was a response to this need for the new,

[11] Paul Johnson, *Enemies of Society* (New York: Atheneum, 1977). See especially chapter 5.

[12] See, for example, Kierkegaard's incisive analysis in "The Present Age," in *A Kierkegaard Anthology*, ed. Robert Bretall (New York: The Modern Library, 1946), pp. 258–69.

for quick meanings which dance lightly on the surface of reality. Social activism is another. The two go hand in hand. It is a proven formula for bringing things to a head quickly.

This is helpful to an understanding of the Christian socialists from a psychological point of view: Maurice, pushing back the conventional boundaries of theology to their mystic limits; Headlam and his fascination for the theater and ballerinas; the French revolutionaries, plunging headlong into the occult and the apocalyptic; Lamennais, tilting at the windmills of Catholicism; Conrad Noel, expelled from Cambridge for heavy drinking and rowdyism, pouring over patristic texts for evidence of revolutionary socialism. Says Peter Jones of Noel: "From his church at Thaxted, which displayed the Red Flag and the green banner of the Sinn Fein, were emitted reverberations of socialism, anti-Sabbatarianism, anti-imperialism, ritualism, and folk art."[13] They were interesting characters, to be sure, with deep fires burning at their core, but oddly dissonant like a chorus singing off-key. In his book on Shaw, G. K. Chesterton wrote that the principles of socialists are unimpeachable but that they go wrong in applying them. I believe the opposite is true. Their principles—concerning human nature, religion, and society—are flawed, but they sometimes apply them in constructive ways. What one admires in them, finally, is their fierce human energies, boiling away against the limits of nature, crying out for expression. The Christian socialist movement is a reminder of how very difficult it is to direct our ideals to creative patterns of action. And we sense instinctively that our world would be less humane had it not existed.

[13] Peter d'A. Jones, *The Christian Socialist Revival 1877–1914* (Princeton: Princeton University Press, 1968), p. 248.

Selected Bibliography

GENERAL BACKGROUND

Beer, Max. *A History of British Socialism*. 2 vols. London: 1919.

Billington, James H., *Fire in the Minds of Men: Origins of the Revolutionary Faith*. New York: Basic Books, 1980.

Cole, G. D. H. *History of Socialist Thought*. 3 vols. London: Macmillan & Co., 1953–1960.

Lichtheim, George. *The Origins of Socialism*. New York: Praeger Publishers, 1969.

ENGLISH CHRISTIAN SOCIALISM

Binyon, Gilbert C. *The Christian Socialist Movement in England*. New York: The Macmillan Co., 1931.

Christensen, Torben. *Origin and History of Christian Socialism 1848–54*. Copenhagen: Universitetsforlaget I Aarhus, 1962.

Jones, Peter d'A. *The Christian Socialist Revival 1877–1914*. Princeton, N.J.: Princeton University Press, 1968.

Raven, Charles E. *Christian Socialism 1848–1854*. New York: Augustus M. Kelley, publishers 1968.

Reckitt, Maurice. *Maurice to Temple: A Century of the Social Movement in the Church of England*. London: Faber & Faber Ltd., 1947.

EUROPEAN CHRISTIAN SOCIALISM

Bowen, Ralph H. *German Theories of the Corporative State*. New York: McGraw-Hill, 1948.

Fogarty, M. *Christian Democracy in Western Europe 1820–1953*. Notre Dame: University of Notre Dame Press, 1957.

BIOGRAPHY

Masterman, Neville C. *John Malcom Ludlow: The Builder of Christian Socialism*. Cambridge: Cambridge University Press, 1963.

Maurice, Frederick, ed. *Life of Frederick Denison Maurice, Chiefly Told through His Own Letters.* 2 vols. London: 1884.

Sheehan, James. *The Career of Lujo Brentano.* Chicago: University of Chicago Press, 1966.

Terrill, Ross. *R. H. Tawney and His Times: Socialism as Fellowship.* Cambridge: Harvard University Press, 1973.

Fletcher, Joseph. *William Temple: Twentieth-Century Christian.* New York: Seabury Press, 1963.

CRITICAL

Craig, Robert. *Social Concern in the Thought of William Temple.* London: Victor Gallancz, 1963.

Lewis, John; Polanyi, Karl; and Kitchin, D. K., eds. *Christianity and the Social Revolution.* London: Victor Gallancz, 1935.

Ulam, Adam E. *Philosophical Foundations of English Socialism.* New York: Octagon Books, 1964.

Selected AEI Publications

Public Opinion, published bimonthly (one year, $18; two years, $34; single copy, $3.50)

Canada at the Polls, 1979 and 1980: A Study of the General Elections, Howard R. Penniman, ed. (426 pp., paper $9.25, cloth $17.25)

The Role of the Legislature in Western Democracies, Norman J. Ornstein, ed. (192 pp., paper $7.25, cloth $15.25)

Liberation South, Liberation North, Michael Novak, ed. (99 pp., $4.25)

British Political Finance, 1830-1980, Michael Pinto-Duschinsky (339 pp., paper $10.50, cloth $17.95)

A Conversation with Michael Novak and Richard Schifter: Human Rights and the United Nations (25 pp., $2.25)

Reconciliation and the Congressional Budget Process, Allen Schick (47 pp., $4.25)

Whom Do Judges Represent? John Charles Daly, mod. (31 pp., $3.75)

The Urban Crisis: Can Grass-Roots Groups Succeed Where Government Has Failed? John Charles Daly, mod. (25 pp., $3.75)

Italy at the Polls, 1979: A Study of the Parliamentary Elections, Howard R. Penniman, ed. (335 pp., paper $8.25, cloth $16.25)

Prices subject to change without notice.

AEI Associates Program

The American Enterprise Institute invites your participation in the competition of ideas through its AEI Associates Program. This program has two objectives:

The first is to broaden the distribution of AEI studies, conferences, forums, and reviews, and thereby to extend public familiarity with the issues. AEI Associates receive regular information on AEI research and programs, and they can order publications and cassettes at a savings.

The second objective is to increase the research activity of the American Enterprise Institute and the dissemination of its published materials to policy makers, the academic community, journalists, and others who help shape public attitudes. Your contribution, which in most cases is partly tax deductible, will help ensure that decision makers have the benefit of scholarly research on the practical options to be considered before programs are formulated. The issues studied by AEI include:

- Defense Policy
- Economic Policy
- Energy Policy
- Foreign Policy
- Government Regulation
- Health Policy
- Legal Policy
- Political and Social Processes
- Social Security and Retirement Policy
- Tax Policy

For more information, write to:

AMERICAN ENTERPRISE INSTITUTE
1150 Seventeenth Street, N.W.
Washington, D.C. 20036